Where the Jobs Are

The Hottest Careers for the '90s

Where the Jobs Are

The Hottest Careers for the '90s

By
Mark Satterfield

CAREER PRESS
180 Fifth Avenue
P.O. Box 34
Hawthorne, NJ 07507
1-800-CAREER-1
201-427-0229 (outside U.S.)
FAX: 201-427-2037

WHERE THE JOBS ARE
THE HOTTEST CAREERS FOR THE '90S

ISBN 1-56414-024-5, $9.95

Cover design by Dean Johnson Design, Inc.
Printed by Bookmart Press

Copies of this volume may be ordered by mail or phone directly from the publisher. To order by mail, please include price as noted above, $2.50 handling per order, and $1.00 for each book ordered. Send to: Career Press, Inc., 180 Fifth Ave., P.O. Box 34, Hawthorne, NJ 07507

Or call Toll-free 1-800-CAREER-1 (in Canada: 201-427-0229) to order using your VISA or MasterCard or for further information on all books published or distributed by Career Press.

Library of Congress Cataloging-in-Publication Data

Satterfield, Mark, 1955-
    Where the jobs are : America's hottest careers for the '90s / by Mark Satterfield.
        p.   cm.
    Includes bibliographical references and index.
    ISBN 1-56414-024-5 : $9.95
    1. Job hunting--United States. 2. Job vacancies--United States. 3. Career Development--United States. 4. Vocational guidance--United States. I. Title.
HF5382.75.U6S3   1992
650.14--dc20
                                   92-13646
                                       CIP

To my wife, Karen, for her unswerving support and encouragement, and to my parents for the same.

Contents

Job Profiles

Contents

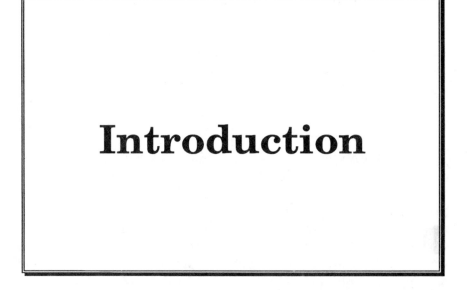

Introduction

The rules for career success have changed. Layoffs are affecting an unprecedented number of white-collar workers. According to some university placement experts, the job market for graduating students is the tightest since the end of World War II. On some campuses, only 20 percent of students have jobs upon graduation. You can't blame students who throw up their hands in despair and conclude that, because there are no jobs, a summer at the beach might be an alternative to an extensive job hunt. A tempting—but bad— idea.

Develop your career survival kit

In the '90s, your career success will be determined by knowing *where* the opportunities are. Now more than ever you will find that you are ultimately responsible for the success of your own career. The perceived security of working for a large corporation is largely an illusion. Today, savvy workers are developing a career survival kit of marketable skills, and knowledge about various career fields.

The time-honored tradition of joining a company right out of school, working diligently and reaping the rewards of your long-term commitment, has been replaced by a more pragmatic and opportunistic career management approach. To succeed in today's competitive arena, you will have to develop a new mindset on how the career game is played.

What's in a name?

For example, one of the traditional symbols of career success has been a job title. Historically, a goal for many individuals was to have the words "vice president" on their business cards. Becoming a vice president was the goal, and success was measured by its attainment. In the '90s you can forget about working for a title. There are many unemployed vice presidents who spent too much time trying to gain this title rather than developing a solid base of marketable business capabilities.

In the '90s employers are less concerned with what you are called than they are with what you can actually *do*. Thus, it is imperative that you develop a repertoire of skills that can be marketed both internally in your company and externally to the business community. You never know when you may be required to conduct a job search. Your business skills and your knowledge of where the jobs are will largely determine your job-search success.

It's never too soon to network...

Another critical component for career survival is developing contacts both inside and outside your company. Although everyone has heard the term "networking," and knows that networking is the method by which most jobs are found, many individuals wait until their jobs are in jeopardy before making an effort to develop business contacts.

...or too late to learn

The role of continuing education in career success is a factor that cannot be underestimated. This does not necessarily mean going to graduate school full time. At a minimum, take courses that will keep you current on developments in your field.

This is especially important for those who are now in a management role. Chances are that you will be more marketable if you retain your technical competence, while at the same time developing strong supervisory skills. You never want to get too far away from the current knowledge in your field. Additionally, by participating in a continuing education program you'll have the opportunity to broaden your base of contacts.

Small companies mean big opportunities

Traditionally, many people limited their career options to just the large Fortune 500 employers. While these companies still offer some excellent opportunities, they represent only a small percentage of the hot jobs in the 1990s.

Since jobs in smaller organizations are often less defined, employees may find themselves working in areas that they did not originally anticipate. This appeals to workers who have broad business interests and can adapt to the flexible nature of smaller companies.

While the 1990s will be a challenge, it's important to keep what you read in the business press in perspective. Doom and gloom tend to generate more ink than sunny skies and clear sailing. Even in the best of times, we never see articles titled "Great Jobs Go Begging." It's always, "Recession Around the Corner, Prepare for Hard Times."

Articles about hiring activity tend to overgeneralize a highly fragmented employment market. Certain industries may be experiencing a slump, but others are successful. Even within a particular industry, certain companies are faring well while others suffer. Good jobs do exist, if you know where to look. And that's exactly what this book is designed to do—give you the knowledge and tools you need to find the hottest career opportunities of the '90s.

The first part of this book details the important job-hunting steps that are crucial to anyone seeking a fulfilling career. In an environment where 80 percent of the available jobs are never advertised, you need to know how to find the jobs in the first place. In Chapter 1, you'll learn about networking—one of the most valuable and effective job-search strategies available to you—and you'll discover some other great resources as well.

Secondly, once you've targeted some prospective companies you might want to work for, I'll show you how to do some important sleuthing in Chapter 2. In order for you to have an edge, you'll have to know as much as possible about your future employer. Where can you find out about the company's principle executives? Its management style and corporate culture? Its organization structure? I'll tell you in Chapter 2.

It can often be a long, torturous journey to get your foot in the door of a prospective employer. Once you do, you certainly don't want to blow it by responding poorly in your interview. Learn how to turn this "make-or-break" step in the job-search process into a job-landing step in Chapter 3.

By the time you've been given a job offer, you may be so grateful you don't care if you have to pay your *employer* a salary! Don't pass up the chance to land a salary you deserve. Learn valuable salary negotiation techniques in Chapter 4.

The second half of the book consists of profiles of some of the hottest careers and fields in the 1990s. Each profile analyzes the field from a variety of aspects. An overview gives you a sense of what day-to-day life is like in the field, what kind of person is best-suited for the work, and what the pros and cons might be. You'll learn what jobs are in demand. You'll learn how to break into the field, what kind of education or training is required and what entry-level opportunities are like. You'll even learn what current entry-level salaries are, as well as mid-level and maximum learning potential.

In addition, I outline a typical career path for each profile, followed by an indication of who and where the major employers in that field are.

Finally, I've included a list of names and addresses of some of the major employers, and industry associations and publications that might be of value to you.

I won't kid you...it's not *easy* to find a good job with a good company—in a good field. But by arming yourself with the necessary knowledge, you *will* discover where the jobs are— and you'll make one of them your own.

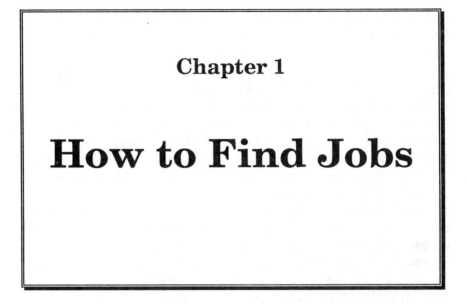

Chapter 1

How to Find Jobs

The job-search process is a game of numbers. The more opportunities you investigate, the greater your chances of success. When most people think about where to find job openings, they consider the want ads in the Sunday paper. But there are many other avenues to find job opportunities. Some of the traditional means include networking and using the services of a recruiting firm.

Your best bet is to take advantage of *all* of these. If you use one method, you're likely to miss out on a lot of opportunities. Let's take a look at each of these resources.

Networking: The power of word of mouth

Most every job seeker has heard about how networking is the most effective means to identify job opportunities. Yet for all the publicity, actually implementing a networking campaign remains a daunting task. "What do I say?" "Who do I contact?" And most frustrating, "How do I overcome this nagging feeling that I'm imposing on the people I'm trying to network with?"

First, let's define our terms. Networking is hardly a magical process that requires special training or unique skills. It is simply the process of using friends, former colleagues and others in your field to help you find a job. You do this by keeping your eyes and ears open to opportunities you hear about, and meeting as many contacts as possible. Since success in the job search is in part driven by statistics, the more people you meet and the more opportunities you hear about, the greater your chances are of finding employment.

One of the key advantages of learning about opportunities through networking is that it often enables you to get a jump on the competition. This becomes apparent when we look at the process by which many companies fill positions. The first step an organization takes is looking internally for a suitable candidate. If no candidate emerges, management will then ask current employees for recommendations. It is at this point that networking pays dividends. If you are referred to the organization by someone you have networked with, you avoid having to compete with the hoards of applicants responding to help-wanted ads and employment agency referrals.

"Who do I contact?"

The key to successful networking is targeting specific companies and meeting as many employees there as possible. There are many different doors that can lead to employment at a company. Your objective is to explore as many as you can.

An initial step is to develop a list of friends, family and business contacts you feel comfortable approaching. It's easy to ask those close to you for contact names in personal meetings—whether at work, over lunch or at family reunions. But most people prefer to initiate the networking process by writing a letter to each contact and then following up on the telephone. The approach that I like is sending a three-page packet, including a cover letter, resume and list of companies you are interested in working for, to each person on your list. The cover letter might read as follows:

As you may have heard, we have recently undergone a major restructuring. Although I've survived the past layoffs, this one caught up with me. Thus, I am now faced with the challenge of investigating new employment opportunities.

At this point I am developing a list of contacts. It occurred to me that within your circle of business and personal acquaintances, you may know of one or more persons who may be interested in receiving my resume. A copy for your perusal is enclosed.

Also enclosed is a list of companies I've researched that could possibly use someone with my background and experience.

I would be grateful if you could share the names of anyone you know in my target companies. Of course, you never know where a new opportunity will turn up, so if you have other contacts that may know of opportunities, I'd welcome their names also.

I'll call you next Tuesday morning to discuss any suggestions you have.

Once your contact gives you a name, discuss the best method of introducing yourself. Ideally your contact would call or write to introduce you, but this is not always feasible. At a very minimum, make sure you have your contact's permission to use his or her name when calling the networking referral.

An effective telephone call to a networking prospect includes the following steps:

1. State who referred you.
2. Explain what type of job you are looking for.
3. Briefly outline why you are qualified.

Networking success depends on your being organized, conise and direct about the purpose of your call. Most people enjoy talking about their profession and are flattered when asked for advice. Moreover, since you are being referred by someone they know and presumably respect, they will usually give you some time. Networking enables you to increase the scope and reach of your job search. It's usually worth the effort.

Recruiting firms: Check them out first

Functioning as intermediaries between applicants and employers, professional recruiting firms have established themselves as important resources for job changers. However the degree of professionalism and competence among recruiting firms varies a great deal. Thus it pays to know how different types of recruiting firms work, and how to find a firm that's right for you.

Although recruiting firms are a viable component of the job-search strategy, you should not put too much reliance on them as the primary source for job leads. It is estimated that recruiting firms fill only 20 percent of the available jobs. Thus, make sure you supplement the use of recruiting firms with other sources, such as newspapers ads and networking.

Be very skeptical of any firm whose fee is not paid by the employer. The recruiting industry has evolved to the point where virtually all reputable firms' fees are paid by the hiring company. You should also be aware of the career marketing firms who advertise that they will introduce you to the "hidden job market." The fee, paid by you, is often substantial, and there has been a great deal of controversy over whether the services they provide are worth the cost.

The recruiting firms you will want to contact fall into two groups: retainer and contingency. In both types of firms, the fee is paid by the employer. However, the method by which they are paid is quite different. This difference is important since it affects your relationship with the firm.

A contingency firm gets paid only if the candidate it refers is actually hired by the employer. This may cause the firm to refer great numbers of candidates hoping that one of the individuals will be selected. Companies may list an opening with many contingency firms since they are only obligated to pay a fee to the firm whose candidate they hire. Thus, there is often a scramble among contingency firms to present as many qualified candidates as they can, as quickly as possible.

This can sometimes make applicants feel that they are simply a product to be bought and sold. Many individuals complain that the contingency recruiters are impersonal and abrupt.

While this varies among agencies, remember that the fee is paid by the employer. The recruiting firm works for the employer, not *you*. Although you should expect the recruiter to be polite, he or she isn't in the business of providing career advice.

Retainer firms, or executive search firms, are paid their fee regardless of whether they fill the job. The retained recruiters liken themselves to other professionals, such as doctors and lawyers, who are paid even if their client is found guilty or the patient does not recover. Their incentive is that if they do not fill the position, it is unlikely that the client will use them again. Typically, retainer firms work on positions paying in excess of $50,000, while contingency firms work on a wide gamut of assignments, where salaries may start at about $15,000.

The key to successfully managing the recruiting firm relationship is finding the right firm and the right recruiter for you. Finding the firms that specialize in your field is relatively easy. *Kennedy Publications* publishes the most comprehensive registry of recruiting firms. Its annual *Directory of Executive Recruiters* has separate sections on contingency and retained recruiters, and lists the firms geographically, by function and industry specializations.

Identifying the right recruiter can be a little trickier. Generally the retained recruiters are older, more experienced managers, and often were executives in the industry they now serve. Since they work on middle-management and senior-level positions, the overwhelming majority are highly professional.

In the contingency ranks, there is a greater disparity in the level of professionalism and experience. Since contingency recruiters work largely on commission, the competition to produce revenues is intense, and turnover is often quite high.

Try to work with a recruiter who has been in the business for at least two years and specializes in your industry. The National Association of Personnel Consultants designates recruiters who have worked for a minimum of two years in the field and have passed an exam. Although many good contingency recruiters do not have the CPC designation, the certification ensures a certain base line of competence.

Take advantage of referrals from friends and business associates. If you identify firms that focus in your field, and work with an experienced recruiter, you will find that recruiting firms can offer valuable assistance to you in your job search.

Classified ads

Help-wanted advertising is one of the more visible sources for job leads. While this makes it easier to identify opportunities, responding to ads places you in direct competition with many other candidates. However, outplacement consultants estimate that somewhere between 15 and 25 percent of all jobs are filled through such ads. So why not increase your job-landing odds by responding to the want ads too?

To better your success, it is important that you look at all of the publications in which a relevant help-wanted ad might appear. In addition to the Sunday newspaper, want ads appear in a variety of trade publications, and business-oriented newspapers such as *The Wall Street Journal,* which runs the majority of its ads on Tuesday. Additionally *The Wall Street Journal* publishes the *National Business Employment Weekly,* a compilation of ads that have appeared in the various regional editions of the *Journal* during the past week. Also, read through the pertinent publications to your industry.

In perusing the Sunday classifieds, read the entire section. Typically, ads are run alphabetically rather than clustered by position or industry. Thus, a candidate seeking a position in Personnel might find a relevant ad appearing in different parts of the classified section under Human Resources, Training, Compensation, Benefits or Management. Many newspapers also publish help-wanted advertising in the business section. These ads are usually directed toward experienced professionals seeking mid-management opportunities.

Help-wanted ads appear in two formats, blind and open. Open ads list the name of the company while blind ads direct you to apply to a post office box. Companies run blind ads for a variety of reasons—and not always to fill a position. In some cases, they may just be trying to get a feeling for what talent is available. Or what salaries people in that position are receiving. If there is a job opening, the position may be confidential, or the company may not want to terminate the incumbent manager until a replacement has been found. If you are currently employed and the description in the blind ad sounds remarkably similar to your job, caution is encouraged.

An additional benefit to companies running blind ads is that they do not have to respond to candidates. Many companies that sell their products to consumers feel obligated to commnicate with all applicants. This can be a burdensome task for some of the larger, better-known corporations.

When responding to help-wanted ads, remember that your letter is likely to be one of hundreds that the company receives. Conciseness is critical.

Many candidates find a three-paragraph strategy to be effective. The first paragraph states how you learned about the position and why your are qualified:

I read with interest your advertisement for a mechanical engineer in last Sunday's Journal Constitution and believe my five years of related technical experience would make me a strong candidate for the position.

Paragraph two discusses your one accomplishment or result that most closely relates to the needs of the employer.

My experience directing the start-up activities of a $1 million distribution center demonstrates my ability to achieve tangible results through managing the activities of a diversified work force.

The third paragraph closes the letter with a statement about what the next step will be. If the name of the employer is given, indicate that you plan to follow up:

I will call you next week to determine the appropriate next step.

In situations where the employer is unknown, you are limited to a more passive closing statement such as:

I look forward to discussing my background with you in the near future.

A common request is for inclusion of salary histories. Although there are differences in opinion on how to respond, a fairly compelling argument can be made *not* to include this information. Salary information is requested by companies as a screening tool. Your strategy is to get the company interested in you before money is discussed. This improves your chances of getting top dollar for your services. Although the ad states that applicants will not be considered unless salary information is included, it is highly unlikely that a qualified candidate would be ruled out.

Are these the only avenues open to the job hunter? Certainly not. While they're some of the most common and effective means of tracking down job openings, there are other methods. For example, say there is a company you'd love to work for. You've done your research and you know that the corporate culture, advancement opportunities and attractive salary potential are for you!

But you can't dig up a contact there. There are no advertised job openings, and the recruiters you've called don't have a relationship with that company. Are you out of luck? Not necessarily. If you've investigated effectively, you should have learned who the company's key contacts or management people are. Your next step is to call or write a specific individual—preferably a manager in the department you're interested in—and ask for an information interview. It's a little trickier getting in without a contact, but it's certainly been done.

If you can approach the contact in a nonpressuring way and clarify that you're not seeking a job but merely advice and expertise, you might get an opportunity to meet. Your approach can be very similar to the one you use with networking contacts. You should emphasize that you're not seeking a job right now, but are requesting advice from an expert on how to further your career. By establishing this new contact, you'll have a foot in the door if a job opening comes up. (Company research and information interviews are further discussed in the next chapter.)

There are other methods to uncover job opportunities. Getting involved in a volunteer capacity in the field you're interested in, joining industry associations, taking advantage of some of computer network programs that advertise job openings or allow job-seekers to advertise of their availability, are a few alternatives. Increase your odds by exploring all the job-finding avenues available.

Chapter 2

Job-Search Success Requires Research

In order for a job search to be successful you must develop a plan. Far too often people jump into the search by attempting to arrange interviews as quickly as possible. This is usually a mistake. If you don't take the time to adequately research the marketplace, you may overlook companies to which you should be applying, and it will be very difficult for you to sell yourself during the interview. Although your initial reaction may be that research isn't necessary, you're likely to find that it is extremely important to the overall success of your job search.

The concept of employment research is often misunderstood and, consequently, a lot of people don't do it very well. Researching a company is different than doing research for a term paper. It's not enough to simply obtain information on the company's financial performance and product lines.

The first step in employment research is to identify all of the potential places where you might work. You're likely to be surprised at the number and variety of companies that could use your skills. To obtain this initial data, head to your local public library. Most libraries have all of the information you'll need; however, they can be a little overwhelming for people who haven't conducted research in a while.

A good first step is to speak to the research librarian. This person is an underutilized resource who can make your time more productive. Research librarians often have master's degrees in library science and are wizards at researching virtually any subject. They can help you quickly find the best reference books on the industries you're interested in.

Some of the reference books you may want to use include:

Dun & Bradstreet's Million Dollar Directory

This five-volume set lists 160,000 public U.S. corporations and 30,000 private companies with a net worth of $500,000 or more. The listings include name, address, telephone number, names and titles of officers and directors, annual sales, number of employees and more.

Standard & Poor's Register of Corporations, Directors and Executives

This series includes a listing of more than 45,000 corporations, including names and titles of officers and directors and the type of information found in the Dun & Bradstreet volumes. Another volume includes biographies of officers, directors, trustees and other key figures in businesses. This information includes their home addresses and association memberships, if available.

Moody's Industry Review

This annual reference, updated weekly, includes 4,000 leading businesses in more than 100 industries and features information about revenues, price-earnings ratios, net income, profit and more.

The Career Guide: Dun's Employment Opprtunities Directory

Another Dun & Bradstreet publication, this directory features companies that have more than 1,000 employees. Listings cover fields such as marketing, sales, computer science and a variety of technical and professional areas. Each listing includes information about what types of occupations are hired, training programs, hiring requirements and more.

Some other valuable resources include the **Encyclopedia of Associations** (lists professional associations by industry and function), **The Guide to American Directories** (describes 330 directories on 400 topics), **Directory of Executive Recruiters** (lists recruiting firms by industry function, location and compensation levels), **Who Owns Whom** (provides information on difficult-to-find companies), **Thomas Register of American Manufacturers** (lists 140,000 product manufacturers), and **Ward's Business Directory of U.S. Private and Public Companies** (lists 133,000 companies).

Once you've identified the companies in your field, your research should take two forms: 1) Identifying the business issues the company faces and determining how your skills would assist the organization in achieving its objectives, and 2) Understanding the management style and culture of the company. Your knowledge of these areas will assist you in presenting yourself as a good "fit" with the organization.

There are a number of ways to obtain this information. First, get a copy of the company's annual report. It is available in many libraries, or may be obtained from the company.

Pay particular attention to the letter in the front. Although the letter from the CEO is often written by the public relations department, it embodies the philosophy of the chief executive. The tone and style of the letter is indicative of the management style of the company. If the letter discusses only financial results and never mentions the development of people, you might surmise that the organization values employees who deliver results, but is not oriented toward management training or teamwork. Depending upon your own personal style this may or may not suit your needs. Certainly this is an area that you would want to explore further in the interview.

Another source of information is your college placement office. Placement offices have company literature available to students or alumni. What's particularly helpful about this information is that it is often specifically recruiting-oriented.

Where the Jobs Are

Many companies prepare brochures, describing what the comany is like to work for, as part of their college recruiting efforts. The placement office can be a gold mine of information. Companies such as the Leo Burnett Advertising Agency, or Kraft, the food manufacturer, have prepared videotapes that give even greater insights into the company culture.

The amount of information available on a company varies. Pubicly traded companies are required to publish more information than closely held private companies. How much information should you have prior to the interview? No one expects you to be privy to internal documents, but recruiters will expect you to know information that is generally available to the public.

Once you've completed your research, it's time to involve other people in your job search. The objective is to find out more information about different jobs and companies. These meetings are often referred to as information interviews.

Your college alumni office is a good source. They can refer you to alumni who are working for a specific company or are in a certain career field. Develop a list of potential contacts, including former co-workers, neighbors, and church and professional association members.

When arranging a meeting, emphasize that you are conducting job research and are *not* trying to set up an interview. Most people will be willing to discuss what they do or answer your questions. However, they are likely to avoid you if they sense that you're trying to hit them up for a job. Try a statement such as: "I've been researching the telecommunications industry and I have a few questions. I was hoping you might have a free hour over the next couple of weeks when I could come by and talk to you."

In the meeting, ask questions about trends in the industry, what skills are in demand and what people like most and least about the company. At the conclusion of the meeting, ask if there is anyone else you should speak with. In this manner, you can become known to people in the industry so that when a job opens up, you are likely to be considered for it.

This investment will pay a tangible dividend when it is time to ask questions during the *real* interview. Unfortunately, many candidates ask superficial questions during the interview. This often can't be helped, since they don't know very much about the company or the industry. However, this leaves the interviewer with the impression that the applicant isn't serious about working for the company. If you've done your research, you have an enormous competitive advantage. Ask questions about what you have concluded are the skills necessary for job success. Ask the recruiter for feedback on your conclusions. Even if you are slightly off the mark, the interviewer will be impressed with the effort you have undertaken.

However, if in the happy event that you land a job interview there, you will show your prospective employer that you are a serious player and not a casual shopper.

Chapter 3

Create a Door-Opening Resume

Resume writing is an imprecise art at best. Given the preponderance of "how-to" information available, it's hardly surprising that writing a resume can be highly confusing. How do you compose a resume that articulates your accomplishments and achievements? How can you make your resume stand out from the masses of paper that employers receive?

Since resumes often arrive in bunches, employers tend to quickly scan the document, seeking out important information. Often a recruiter will spend less than 20 seconds reviewing a resume. Thus the key in having your resume pass this initial screen is to make sure the relevant information about your professional experiences, accomplishments and achievements can be easily found.

What to cut

Nonessential information that does *not* compel the reader to invite you in for an interview should be eliminated. Individuals often provide far too much information. Remember that the mission of the resume is to get you an interview. Anything that does not contribute to that primary purpose should be eliminated. This would include the following:

Personal information. Height, weight, eye color. This type of information takes up space and can cause a recruiter to rule you out if one number is out of proportion to the other. Similarly, your health is assumed to be fine and does not need to be mentioned. Although we are all proud of our children, Buffy's and Scooter's ages and health are of little interest to recruiters. Don't indicate your marital status. If you say you're married, the company may assume you are stable—or may conclude that you cannot travel or relocate in the future. Since you don't know how the reader will react, it's best to leave it off.

Salary history. Negotiating your salary is a sensitive process. Putting your salary information on your resume tips your hand too early in the employment process. Including salary information also allows recruiters to rule you out before they learn about your skills and accomplishments. If you are asked on an employment application about salary de-mands, simply write in "negotiable" or "open."

Reasons you left past employers. A resume is not a confessional. However, some writers feel compelled to include the most damaging information on their resumes. Reasons why you left past employers are often complex and difficult to condense into one or two sentences. This area is best discussed in the interview.

References. The ubiquitous tag line, "references will be furnished upon request," states the obvious. Rather than putting references on your resume, you should prepare a separate sheet with names and contact information. It is highly unlikely that your references will be called until after a job interview.

Other. Putting the word RESUME at the top states the obvious and takes up space. Unless you are applying for a model or acting assignment, including a photo is inappropriate. Avoid listing controversial or dangerous activities in the "Additional Information" section. Rappelling or parachuting may be perfectly acceptable hobbies, however they may cause a prospective employer concern.

Which format is best?

Individuals often wonder about how to organize the information on their resumes. What's the best format? It depends. There are a number of acceptable formats. If you have employment gaps in your work history or are seeking to change fields, a functional resume may be your best bet. This type of resume focuses on key areas of responsibility such as technical skills or supervisory experience. Employment dates are either omitted or appear on the bottom of the resume. While this format can sometimes be helpful if there are gaps in your employment history, many employers are quite leery of it.

The most popular format is a chronological resume. Your work experience is presented in reverse chronological order starting with your most current job. This format is suitable for most people. You should focus the greatest amount of space on your past 10 years of experience. Individuals with many years of employment may wish to cluster earlier experience under a general heading of "Previous Experience." Although it is not etched in stone that all resumes must be one page, try to keep yours to no more than two pages.

It's important that you focus on your accomplishments and achievements, rather than your responsibilities. Employers are more interested in what you accomplished—they want to know your results—so they can determine that *you'll* be an asset for *them*. Putting together your list of accomplishments is often the most difficult part of developing a resume. However it is worth the investment of time.

Accomplishments do not have to be limited to those in which an entire department was reorganized or a new product line introduced. What employers are looking for are people who consistently make contributions. Was your department better off by having had you as an employee, or did you simply collect dust? In reflecting on your prior jobs think about what you organized, created, established, initiated, developed, supervised, designed, saved, increased or improved. This exercise can help stimulate your thinking.

A resume is simply an advertisement. It doesn't generate job offers, it generates interviews. To the extent you develop a resume that focuses on your accomplishments and achievements, and eliminates nonessential information, the greater your odds are of standing out in the pack—opening the doors that will lead to interviews and job offers.

Following are just a few resume books that may help you develop your door-opening resume:

> *Your First Resume, Third Edition*, by Ron Fry (Career Press, 1992).
>
> *The Smart Woman's Guide to Resumes and Job Hunting,* by Betsy Sheldon and Julie Adair King (Career Press, 1991).
>
> *Resumes That Knock 'Em Dead,* by Martin Yate (Bob Adams Inc., 1992).
>
> *Resumes! Resumes! Resumes!,* by the editors of Career Press (Career Press, 1992).
>
> *Encyclopedia of Job-Winning Resumes,* by Myra Fournier and Jeffrey Spin (Round Lake Publishing, 1992).

Chapter 4

Interviewing

Although Woody Allen once said that 90 percent of life was just showing up, success in the interview depends upon more. Succeeding in the interview depends on adapting your style to different interviewers, being prepared for the common questions, not getting thrown by trick questions, and asking insightful questions. The interview is where the sale is made. Since it's likely that the recruiter is interviewing a lot of candidates, you've got to make sure that you don't get lost in the crowd. In this chapter, we will examine some of the components of the interview and ways to increase your odds of successfully landing an offer.

Interviewing with different levels

A candidate rarely interviews with just one person if the prospective employer is interested in that individual. A common mistake is to assume that there is one key decision-maker, and that everyone else is superfluous. This is seldom true.

Where the Jobs Are

Although each interviewer has a different level of hiring authority, most of them can effectively veto the candidate. Thus, the more people you can positively influence, the greater your likelihood of receiving an offer. Successful applicants often share one trait: Like all skilled communicators they tailor their remarks to their audience. The conversation they have with the personnel manager tends to be quite different from their interview with the direct supervisor. Typically, there are three types of people you will meet: a human resources recruiting manager, the boss and the *boss's* boss.

The first person you're likely to meet is the human resources recruiting manager. This person's major objective is to ensure a certain level of quality in all candidates referred beyond him or her. In assessing your background, the recruiting manager typically looks for specific experiences or technical skills

In addition to screening for technical competency, the recruiter also will assess your "fit" with the company. When interviewers are determining fit, they are attempting to answer a variety of highly subjective questions such as; "To what extent is your way of doing things compatible with the way we do things here?" or "How likely are you to be motivated by our system of rewards?" While there is no benefit in attempting to be someone you are not, if your research indicates that the company is your kind of place, tell the recruiting manager why you think you represent a good fit.

When interviewing with the recruiting manager, you should tailor your questions to cover the broad parameters of the job. Examples include: "Why is this job open?" "Why are you filling the position externally?" "What happened to the incumbent?" "What are the major accountabilities of the position?" These questions will help you assess the opportunity.

Ultimate responsibility for the selection decision rests with the boss. This interview is usually the most technically oriented, as the boss attempts to determine if you can actually perform the duties of the position. You should do everything you can to speak the unique language of the job. You'd better know the buzzwords, and use them. Remember, your goal in this interview is to develop the boss's confidence in your capability to do the job. If you succeed in this specific mission, chances are you will get an offer.

The boss is the best person to ask about the specifics of the position. Although this sounds obvious, it's surprising how many times I've heard about the superficiality of applicant questions. Key areas to cover here include: "What criteria will my performance be measured against?" "How will I receive feedback about my work?" "Where can the job lead?"

If the other interviews go well, you will meet the boss's boss. Sometimes this person is a key decision-maker, other times a rubber stamp. He or she determines if the candidate is capable of assuming additional responsibilities.

When asking questions, the perspective of the interviewer should be kept in mind. The boss's boss has a unique vantage point from which the following types of issues can be addressed: career path, accountabilities of the job and the influence of business trends on the company and the position.

While no single strategy can guarantee success in the interiewing process, you can increase your chances of getting an offer if you can identify the perspective of the different interviewers, and tailor your presentation to meet them.

Three most frequently asked questions

While no two interviews are exactly the same, there are certain questions that are asked frequently. Let's take a look at three of the most common questions and some of the tricky questions that you'll want to watch for.

1."Tell me a little about yourself." A difficult question to answer because it is so open-ended. It is important that you focus on the aspects of your background that most relate to the needs of the employer. You don't want to spend precious time on areas in which the interviewer has little interest. Unfortunately, this question provides few clues as to what the interviewer is interested in. Thus, candidates sometimes respond by giving long-winded answers that bore the interviewer and don't address the important parts of their background.

This question can be best handled in one of two ways. The first is to prepare and have rehearsed an overview of your background. Your presentation may begin with a sentence or two about where you were brought up, but should quickly move to colleges attended and your professional work experience. Focus on your key accomplishments and the skills you would bring to a new employer. Try to keep this verbal summary of your background to under three minutes.

Practice articulating your answer. There is a big difference between thinking through an answer and act-ally speaking it. The more you practice, the more succinct you will become.

The second method of addressing this question is to provide a brief synopsis of your background, and then throw the question back to the interviewer. This is a very effective strategy for individuals with extensive work experience. An example might be: "Well, as you can see from my resume, I graduated from Georgia Tech with a degree in electrical engineering, worked for a number of years in the high technology field, and for the past three years have worked for the XYZ consulting company. Which of these would you like for me to talk about first?" The interviewer's response will tell you which area of your background is of most interest.

2."What are your strengths and weaknesses?" Obviously it is much easier to answer the first part of this question. However, provide a specific example to back up your claim. Anyone can say that dealing with people under pressure is a strength. By providing a concrete example of *when* you demonstrated this skill, you will convince the interviewer that this is truly one of your assets.

Talking about a weakness will not hurt your candidacy if you also discuss the steps you are taking to improve in this area. Discuss a weakness that is both common and correctable, such as public speaking. "One of the areas my boss mentioned I needed to work on is making group presentations. To improve in this area, I enrolled in the Toastmasters Presentation Workshop and actively sought out opportunities to speak before groups. Although today I'm not someone who's ready to tackle Broadway, I do feel that I am able to express myself persuasively and concisely."

Another strategy is to respond with what is really considered a strength. For example, "When I sink my teeth into a project, I become a workaholic until it's completed. I know my pace can be difficult to others who work with me, and I try to be sensitive to their pace. But it's hard for me to suppress my enthusiasm when I'm doing something I love."

3. "What type of salary are you seeking?" This question is often asked not only to determine if the company can afford you, but as a trick question. Its purpose is to determine if you're driven by money or the opportunity. A good answer shows that you're the type of employee who values opportunity first, but expects to be paid a competitive wage. For example:

"Well Mr. Recruiter, like everyone else in the world, I want to make as much money as possible. However, I believe my long-term satisfaction will be determined more by the challenges and the opportunities than by the initial starting salary." Since you don't want to be low-balled, you might add: "I would expect to be paid a salary competitive with what my counterparts at other firms make."

If the recruiter persists in knowing your demands, you have little choice but to name a figure. You should always research the job marketplace prior to an interview to determine your competitive market value. Talk with colleagues, executive recruiters or the placement director at your school. Using your research, articulate your requirements in a range of $4,000 to $6,000. Speaking in ranges increases the likelihood that you won't rule yourself out or be paid less than you deserve. Whatever range you give, make sure the lowest figure you give is one that is truly acceptable to you.

Dealing with those "tricky" questions

You've also got to be prepared for the trick questions that are commonly asked. These are the questions containing a hidden agenda. Sometimes that agenda is subtle; other times it is overt. Regardless, it's important that you be on the lookout for trick questions and have your answers prepared. Let's examine some of the more common trick questions, discuss why they are asked, and review some of the strategies you might consider in answering them.

Where the Jobs Are

1. "What's your opinion of your fellow co-workers?" Interviewers often ask you this to see if you will speak negatively about your business associates. They figure that if you criticize your co-workers, you're likely to be a negative influence. Thus, regardless of your personal opinion of your fellow workers, mention only positive attributes. Remember that the interview is a sales situation and not a confessional.

2. "Who was the boss you had the most difficulty working with?" Again, the attempt is being made to get you to speak negatively about an individual. If you talk about the differences in opinion or management style you and your boss had, you'll come across as defensive. Answer this question by articulating what you learned from the experience. If you can discuss how you grew as an employee as a result of working for the individual, you'll greatly impress the interviewer.

3. "How many hours a week do you have to work in order to accomplish your job?" Be careful. Candidates sometimes trip themselves up by stating that they work an excessive number of hours. This can leave the impression that if only you worked more efficiently, you would accomplish more. An effective way to answer this question is to approach it from the standpoint that your job is never truly complete.

"Given the nature of my work, it's possible that I could devote every waking hour to the job and still have opportunities left unexplored. I think what is important is knowing how to focus on the important issues and not get overly involved in the minutia associated with the project. I find that, to a certain extent, I never completely stop thinking about work; in fact, I often get good ideas after I leave the office."

4. "How long will you stay with us?" Obviously the company is looking for a level of commitment and wants to avoid job-hoppers. However, going overboard and committing yourself as an indentured servant is silly and probably won't be believed. In answering this question, focus on the challenge of the assignment. "One of the things that attracted me to this company is the feeling that this assignment will be very challenging. Contributing to the growth of the organization is very important to me. As long as I remain challenged, I would not anticipate wanting to seek employment elsewhere."

5. "Are you willing to relocate?" If you are interviewing for a branch office assignment, this question is often asked to determine if you are willing to eventually relocate to the company's headquarters. This is an issue for companies such as Pizza Hut where all roads eventually lead to Wichita. Other times, the question is asked to determine your willingness to make sacrifices in the company's interest. In preparation for this question, research where the company's headquarters and major facilities are. If you're dead-set against relocating, it's best to be honest. But, be prepared for the consequences.

6. "What aspects of your job do you considered to be the most critical?" This is usually asked to determine your ability to differentiate the important from the mundane. Answer this question by focusing on those aspects that either help build the business or contribute to the bottom line. There are compelling business reasons why you were hired. Articulate those critical components.

Keep in mind that there are often multiple agenda items associated with seemingly straightforward questions. Think about what you think the interviewer is trying to get at, and answer accordingly.

How not to be forgotten

Few people actually blow the interview. However, they fail to impress the interviewer with their capabilities, and are easily forgotten. This often occurs because individuals talk in generalities rather than articulating specific achievements. Describing your past experiences by using stories or anecdotes is one of the most effective means of impressing an interviewer.

Using stories to describe your accomplishments helps you to stand out and be remembered, because we remember examples better than we remember facts. Thus, if you list a string of strengths, nobody will remember what you said 15 minutes after you leave the interview. Moreover, by simply articulating a laundry list of strengths you are not backing up your claim. By describing situations in which you demonstrated those strengths, you will convince the interviewer that you possess them. And you will have a higher probability of being remembered after the interview.

Telling stories about your background is a skill. Some people are naturally good at it while others are not. However, it is a skill that most people can master with a little practice. The trick is to establish a format for your anecdotes that will enable you to avoid being too brief or overly long-winded. The acronym *STAR* (*Situation, Task, Action* and *Result*) is often helpful in providing this framework.

First, think about a *situation* or *task* that you faced. Describe this situation in two or three sentences. This establishes the background for your story.

Next, describe the *action* that you took. At this stage, it is important that you speak about what you did specifically. There is a tendency for candidates to gloss over their accomplishments. While you don't want to appear arrogant, you do want to take credit for the role that you played.

Conclude your anecdote by describing the *result* you achieved. Discuss how your work helped your employer. Try to discuss the result in measurable or quantifiable terms.

For example, an accountant described a time in which an accounting system he was expected to implement quickly was threatened by a manager who was slow to commit his support. To convince the manager to support the accountant's effort, the accountant proposed a 7 a.m. meeting to discuss the project. Both this presentation and the accountant's willingness to meet so early impressed the manager, who gave his approval. The accounting system was then quickly implemented. As a result, the system decreased by 25 percent the time it took to process invoices.

Pretend you were the interviewer who just heard the anecdote from the accountant. You would probably think of the accountant in such positive terms as *action-oriented, hard-working, detail-oriented* and *resourceful*. You would remember this anecdote, and the accountant, for some time to come.

Identifying the *right* stories to tell is a critical step. You will want to prepare an array of anecdotes that can be deployed as needed during the interview. The first step is to compile a list of situations or activities in which you have been successful.

These can relate to work, school or other outside interests. You should be able to come up with an initial list of at least 30. For each one of these *situations* or *tasks*, write out the corresponding *action* that you took and the *result* you achieved. Don't worry if you can't quantify all of your results. While it makes for a more impressive story if you can, sometimes the result is simply that the project was completed on time.

A final step before the interview is to put yourself in the interviewer's shoes. If you were hiring someone for this job, what types of skills would you be looking for? Write them down. Review your list of anecdotes to identify which stories demonstrate your skills in those areas.

Finally, practice articulating your accomplishments out loud. There is a difference between *thinking* how you will say something and actually saying it. By working on preparing and articulating your anecdotes, you increase your chances of standing out in a positive way while your competition becomes a blur in the employer's mind.

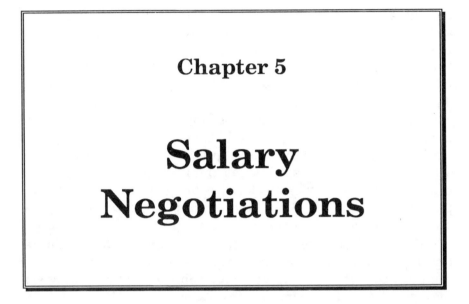

Chapter 5

Salary Negotiations

Congratulations! You got a job offer! Before you say yes, however, you need to complete one more important step in the job-landing process. You must discuss compensation terms. Chances are you may feel that you don't have the luxury of being demanding. You may be satisfied with the salary you were offered. But before you sign on the dotted line, be sure you understand—and agree to—the terms of your salary package.

While salary is seldom the primary reason why you will accept or decline a position, it certainly is of considerable importance. However, salary is only one component of the total compensation package, and savvy job seekers realize that it pays to fully investigate all of the compensation components. When you receive an offer of employment, you may wish to consider negotiating the following:

Bonuses. Participating in the company's bonus plan is one common way to increase your total compensation. Bonuses are usually paid based on a combination of factors including overall company performance, specific business unit performance and individual performance. Bonuses are typically a percentage of your base salary and can range from 10 percent to 100 percent. In larger organizations, participation in the bonus pool is largely determined by management level and may not be negotiable. However, in smaller companies that do not have rigid policies on who may receive a bonus, this may be worth negotiating.

Stock Options. You may be able to acquire a specified number of shares at a pre-established price within a specific time frame. Historically, stock options were only granted to senior-level individuals. This has changed in recent years. For example, PepsiCo has introduced a program in which all employees receive stock. Since stock options are potentially lucrative, you should discuss them in the salary negotiation process.

Signing Bonuses. One issue that companies face when recruiting managers is salary compression. It is difficult for a company to justify paying you more than they pay existing employees who perform similar jobs. In order to attract qualified candidates, many companies offer a signing bonus. This enables the candidate to achieve his or her compensation objectives without upsetting the existing salary structure.

Relocation Allowance. If your new job requires moving to a new location, make sure you thoroughly investigate the relocation program. At a minimum, most companies will provide for the physical move. Additional costs may include increased insurance coverage on your transported furniture, a house-hunting trip, temporary living accommodations, and expenses incurred while you make the transition to your new house.

The amount of money provided to cover expenses, such as deposits for the phone, gas and electric companies, and the installation of carpets and draperies varies. Typically, renters are given a sum equal to two weeks' salary, and homeowners are offered a month's salary. However, this is negotiable, so it pays to investigate. If you are relocating, make sure the company sends you its relocation package that will provide you with an overview of how the company will assist you in the move.

Accelerated Review. If the offered salary is lower than you wanted, but you are excited about the opportunity, ask for an accelerated review date. Typically, employees are reviewed and their salaries are adjusted annually. However, companies are often willing to review your performance in three or six months. This gives you an opportunity to demonstrate your capabilities, prove your value to the organization, and reap financial rewards, without waiting an extended period of time.

Benefits. A company's benefit program is one of the least important issues in the compensation package. As benefits are becoming more expensive, the differences between the programs provided have diminished. Today, benefit packages cover most of the expenses incurred when you are ill, and you share the cost. Although your cost is significantly less than if you were to purchase the insurance on your own, it can still be a substantial sum.

Pay attention to companies offering "cafeteria benefit programs." This allows you to choose, from among an array of services, those that best meet the needs of yourself and your family. Most benefit programs offer the option of long-term disability insurance, which you should consider.

Should you accept lower pay?

You might be faced with the issue of whether to accept a lower salary in a new position. This is confronting more and more job changers. There are no simple answers; outplacement consultants and career advisers state that there are compelling reasons both for and against accepting a lower salary.

Making the right salary decision is dependent upon knowing your market value. There are a number of methods to determine this. Co-workers are a valuable source of information, although it is important to differentiate between what your co-workers *think* they should be making and true market value.

Two impartial sources are executive recruiting firms and university placement offices. Since executive recruiters earn their livings by keeping their fingers on the pulse of the employment marketplace, they are valuable resources. When discussing your compensation with a recruiter, make sure he or she specializes in your field. Some of the larger firms, such as accounting recruiter Robert Half International, Inc. periodically publish salary surveys that are available upon request.

Where the Jobs Are

The decision to accept a lower salary makes sense if you are changing careers. In most cases, compensation directly relates to the amount of experience you have. Walking away from your "career equity" by changing careers will normally result in a lower salary. Accepting a lower salary is the ultimate test of how committed you are to changing professions. For some people this financial sacrifice is worth it.

Finally, accepting a lower salary makes sense in situations where you can receive an additional form of compensation. An example might be taking a smaller salary in exchange for an equity or ownership opportunity. Individuals pursuing sales or marketing positions often work for a small base salary, but have the potential to earn more money through bonuses and commissions. If you are considering such an opportunity, make sure you fully understand how the bonuses are computed and how much you can expect to earn in your first year.

Also, if you're relocating to another part of the country, you should determine whether the salary you're considering is truly lower. You may discover that the cost of living is also lower. By making a move and taking a cut, you may be getting a raise!

It seldom makes sense to accept less money if you are employed and being recruited by another company. If you are in this position, you can expect the competing firm to make it worth your while to change jobs. Keep in mind that you are in a strong negotiating position, and don't compromise too early.

In fact, compromising too early on salary is one of the major sources of frustration for many job changers. While you should not have unrealistic salary expectations, you also shouldn't sell yourself short. This is particularly true for individuals who have been laid off. Since being laid off can greatly affect your self esteem, an unfortunate reaction is to settle for less money than you can legitimately command. In these situations, as you settle into the new job and the financial compromise becomes economic reality, job dissatisfaction can result. This often affects job performance and can prove disastrous.

Interestingly, there is a considerable amount of logic to support the contention that most employers will not intentionally low-ball you on salary. The reason is that recruiting and hiring are enormously time-consuming and expensive tasks. Thus, once the arduous work of interviewing has been completed, the greatest fear of the employer is that the newly hired individual will quit. Offering a salary considerably below the current market is an invitation for employee turnover.

In order to determine what salary is right for you, find out what your market value is. Be realistic but don't compromise too quickly, and remember that total compensation is more than just the base salary you receive. By being aware of the other components, you may find that you will have the opportunity to increase the value of the total financial package.

Job Profiles

Where the Jobs Are

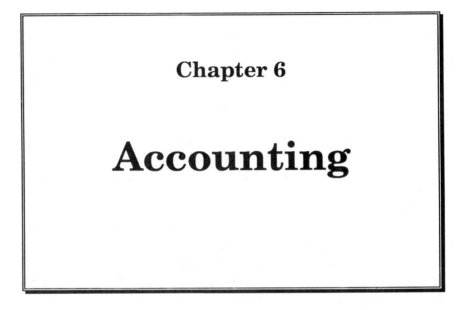

Chapter 6

Accounting

As the saying goes, those who think accountants aren't creative do their own taxes. The stereotypical image of the acounant as the green-eyeshade bean-counter is obsolete. Today's accountant plays an integral and important role in business and industry. As one manager put it, "You *listen* to your lawyer, but you *do* what your accountant tells you to do."

Accountants will most often work for either a corporation or an accounting firm. In a CPA firm accountants work in either the tax or audit areas. All publicly held companies are required to have an annual audit of their finances by a certified public accounting firm. The work requires someone who is extremely detailed and meticulous. Auditors review the company's books to ensure that both the money coming in and going out is properly accounted for. The work is very appealing to people with an investigative orientation. Auditors often trace sums of money through a series of complex financial transactions.

Auditors have a lot more interaction with people than you might guess. Developing good relationships with the clients is critical for success. Interpersonal skills are important since many clients fear the auditors. Although most companies get a clean bill of health, there is always the possibility that the audtors will unearth something bad about the company. Thus, sometimes clients resist giving auditors necessary financial records. To overcome companies' perceptions that auditors are "out to get them,"auditors must avoid ruffling feathers and maintain integrity.

Working as a tax accountant is the closest thing to total job security. The tax code is complex and it changes frequently. Tax considerations play a major role in many decisions made by individuals and corporations.

Tax accountants are more research-oriented than their audit area counterparts. The rules change so frequently that they must continually update their knowledge. Tax questions must be researched extensively before opinions are given. Investigative skills and an interest and capacity for research are important for success.

Tax accountants spend a great deal of time making judgment decisions. While some deductions are blatantly illegal, there are a lot of gray areas in the tax code. Written rules can be interpreted in ways not originally intended. How far to go in interpreting the rules is a judgment skill that tax accountants must develop. They spend considerable time advising clients on various strategies, ranging from conservative to aggressive. What you can get away with without invoking the ire of the IRS is the art of the tax accountant.

Corporate accountants play an invaluable role as advisers to management on the company's financial well-being. They may be involved in issues such as financing, collections, payables and receivables or cost analysis. Corporate accountants manage the activities of the outside CPA firm and other financial consultants. Their work requires them to interface with many departments within the company.

What's hot and why

Auditors. CPA firms need qualified auditors since all public companies must be audited. The profession suffers from higher-than-average turnover, which makes entry-level opportunities plentiful. Because of travel demands, many auditors leave their firms after one or two years to pursue graduate degrees or to work for client companies. Thus the firms must be aggressive in creating a pipeline of people to fill these positions. The field is highly respected, compensates well, and provides excellent training. The skills you learn as an auditor are beneficial in many different career fields.

Tax accountants. It's hard to identify a field in which there is more demand or job security. Since tax accounting is a highly specialized practice, most people stay in the field their entire careers. The only downside to the tax area is that it may be difficult to transfer out of. However, it is enormously challenging and can be very financially rewarding. You must make a commitment to the field and be willing to invest time in continually updating yourself on the changes in the tax code. As long as death and taxes are the two certainties in life, tax accountants will be in demand.

Corporate accountants. Demand is strong, primarily at the entry level since CPA firms scoop up so many of the accounting majors. Many college graduates don't even think about starting their careers in industry, thus a lot of jobs go unfilled. You'll probably have to approach the companies yourself since many of them don't come on campus. A corporate accounting career offers less travel than working for a CPA firm, but provides more opportunity to develop extensive relationships with co-workers. Additionally, you'll benefit from working with a lot of different departments and developing a broad business perspective.

Breaking in

Whether you choose to go into auditing, tax accounting or corporate accounting, you'll need an undergraduate degree in accounting. Tax accountants often get a graduate degree in business, tax or law before entering the field. Since the licensing process for accountants is quite strict, you'll normally have to decide by the beginning of your junior year to pursue an accounting track. If you can't meet the requirements as an undergraduate, there are a number of graduate programs that can give you the necessary credits. You can get details by calling the admissions office at your local college or university.

If you are going to work in a CPA firm—as either an auditor or a tax accountant—you'll also have to get your CPA certification within your first five years of employment. The CPA exam tests your knowledge in four areas; law, audit, theory and practice. Normally, your firm will enroll you in one of the preparation courses that are very helpful. You can pass the exam in increments, but your career will be limited until you're successful. After passing the exam and working for two years (in most states) you can sign your name to an audit statement as a CPA.

Individuals pursuing a career as a corporate accountant don't usually obtain a CPA. The advanced degree of choice is an MBA, which can open doors within the corporation. People enter corporate accounting jobs at various points in their career. Corporations hire people at entry level, mid- management and senior levels. By contrast, most people enter an accounting firm at the entry level.

The bulk of entry-level jobs with CPA firms are staffed by on-campus recruiting. However, the firms, especially the smaller ones, often hire people who apply directly. Listings of accounting firms in your area can be found through the yellow pages, local chamber of commerce or your local chapter of the National Association of CPAs.

Corporate accounting jobs are found in newspaper ads or by applying directly to the company. The best days for ads are Sunday and Monday. Make sure you read the entire help-wanted section since jobs in accounting aren't limited to listings under "Accountant." Major companies in your area can be found through your local chamber of commerce.

Recruiters put a lot of emphasis on grades. If your grades are below a 3.5 on a 4.0 scale, you may have difficulty hooking up with one of the large national firms. Consider retaking a class to bring up the grade or focus on the regional and local firms. Corporations tend not to place as much emphasis on grades. They often are more willing to give applicants a chance if they appear interested in the company and can demonstrate that they willing to work hard.

Interviewers place a lot of weight on interpersonal skills. This is especially true for auditors and corporate accountants. Be prepared to discuss the specifics of why you're interested in the employer and why you want to be an accountant. The recruiters will also focus on your leadership skills, and they particularly like people who have a diversity of interests.

Compensation

Entry-level salaries for auditors and tax accountants at the large national firms average $26,000. You can earn another 10 percent to 15 percent through overtime. Entering the field with a graduate degree usually adds $6,000 to $7,000 to the base salary. Opportunities with smaller accounting firms and corporations pay less. Corporations generally don't offer overtime. However, the corporate accountant usually doesn't have to travel as much as the auditor.

Five years into the career, the accountant with the firm will earn approximately $35,000 to $38,000. A partner in a large firm will earn six figures. It usually takes up to 12 years to become a partner. The corporate accountant can earn similar money at the vice president level.

Career path

The career path in a large accounting firm is fairly structured: staff accountant-to-senior accountant-to-supervisor-to-manager-to-senior manager-to-partner. At the supervisor level, you begin to have responsibility for managing other accountants. At the manager level you'll be expected to direct major portions of a client engagement and have extensive client contact. You must demonstrate business development skills in order to become a partner.

The corporate accounting career is more varied. You may be rotated through a series of jobs, which expose you to the areas of cost, accounts payable, accounts receivable and finance. The head accountant in a company is the controller or vice president. This level can be reached in 8 to 10 years in a smaller company, or 12 to 15 years in a major corporation.

Major employers: Who and where

Accounting careers aren't limited to any one area of the country. Thus accounting is one of the more portable careers. The accounting firms are dominated by the Big Six, which include: Price Waterhouse & Co., Deloitte & Touche, Ernst & Co., Arthur Andersen & Co., Peat Marwick Main & Co., and Coopers & Lybrand. Good regional and local firms exist in every city. They can be found in a variety of reference books in your library, the yellow pages and through your local chapter of the National Association of CPAs.

Positions in corporate accounting exist in virtually every mid-sized and large company. Call your local chamber of commerce to get a major employers list for your city. This will give you an overview of the companies you might want to apply to. The local office of the National Association of Accountants can also be a helpful resource.

Resources

Some key employers

Arthur Andersen & Co.
69 W. Washington Street
Chicago, IL 60602
312-580-0069

Ernst & Co.
100 Wall Street
New York, NY 10005
212-747-3500

Coopers & Lybrand
1251 Avenue of the Americas
New York, NY 10020
212-536-2000

Peat Marwick Main & Co.
3 Chestnut Ridge Road
Montvale, NJ 07645
201-307-7756

Deloitte & Touche
10 Westport Road
Wilton, CT 06897
203-761-3000

Price Waterhouse & Co.
1251 Avenue of the Americas
New York, NY 10020
212-489-8900

Associations

American Accounting Association
5717 Bessie Drive
Sarasota, FL 33583
813-921-7747

National Associations of Accountants
10 Paragon Drive
Montvale, NJ 07645-1760
201-573-9000

American Institute of Certified Public Accountants
1211 Avenue of the Americas
New York, NY 10036
212-575-6200

National Society of Public Accountants
1010 North Fairfax Street
Alexandria, VA 22314
703-549-6400

Publications

Accounting News
Warren, Gorham & Lamont, Inc.
One Penn Plaza
New York, NY 10119
212-971-5000

Accounting Today
Lebhar-Friedman
425 Park Avenue
New York, NY 10022
212-371-9400 ext. 440

Journal of Accountancy
1211 Avenue of the Americas
New York, NY 10036
212-575-6200

The CPA Journal
200 Park Avenue, 10th Floor
New York, NY 10166-0010
212-973-8300

National Public Accountant
National Society of Public
Accountants
1010 North Fairfax Street
Alexandria, VA 22314
703-549-6400

New Accountant
New DuBois Corporation
33 Village Square
Glen Cove, NY 11542
516-759-3484

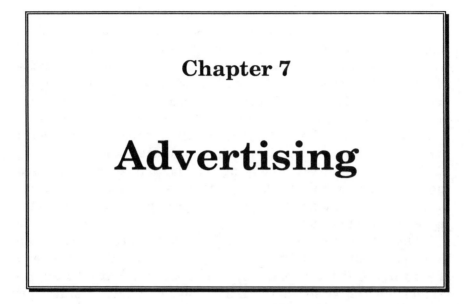

Chapter 7

Advertising

There is, perhaps, no other business that so greatly influences our daily life. Our choices regarding the type of car we drive, the beer we drink and the clothes we wear are all influenced by advertising. As a career, advertising offers a unique blend of opportunities. In few other industries will you find a more eclectic group of individuals all under one roof. Yet the public's perception of advertising is often based on the bumbling antics of television's Darren Stevens of "Bewitched." Nothing could be further from the truth.

The advertising business is a service profession. Getting and keeping clients is the name of the game. If you have no clients, you have no business. Since clients can and do switch agencies frequently, there is a strong competitive spirit in the advertising industry. Advertising is driven by the continued search for the next big idea. What will excite the client? What will make the public go out and buy this product?

Hot advertising jobs are in two areas; people who work on creating advertising and people who manage the relationship between the agency and the client.

Ad writers and artists often work in cubicles or in a bullpen environment. This encourages interaction and some horseplay. Agencies encourage this environment since it stimulates creativity. Some artists and writers do their best work early in the morning while others work best late at night. Agencies try to accommodate these employees by limiting the number of rules on dress codes and office hours. Although the environment is informal and at times somewhat zany, there is enormous pressure on the artists and writers to produce results.

Creating an ad is challenging. The ad you see on television must conform to the marketing strategy set out by the company. The ad must manipulate the perception the consumer has about the product.

While the writers and artists create the advertisements, the account executives are the primary points of contact between the agency and the client. Account executives have an appreciation for the creative process involved in advertising, but their skills are quite different.

Account executives are consultants. They advise clients on the role of advertising in the clients' marketing strategy. A good account executive is more than just an information carrier between the client and the creative team. Successful account executives play an integral role in helping the client develop the marketing strategy. Since account executives are experts on consumer behavior, they can provide insights that the client does not have.

What's hot and why

Most advertising people wouldn't want to work in another industry. Despite the competitiveness and the stress, the ad business is a lot of fun. If you're a writer or an artist, advertising lets you apply your creative skills daily and get paid for it. If you're business-oriented but want to work in a creative environment, advertising offers a unique blend of the practical and the innovative.

Advertising agencies need people who can work well with clients. The ability to communicate equally effectively with buttoned-up marketing executives and creative directors is a unique skill. Good account executives are always in de-mand.

Since advertising is about ideas, the business is always looking for a person who can express a concept in a new or innovative way. If you are fascinated by what makes a person buy one product over another, advertising is the place to be.

The advertising field is intense, and competition fierce. Ad agencies, large and small, confront a constant state of flux. A major client pulls the account, and it may result in serious cutbacks. Thus, job security in advertising is often an oxymoron.

But as long as our society is market-driven—and it certainly appears that it will remain that way—there is an important place for those advertising professionals who are talented, hard-working, creative and willing to go where the work is.

Breaking in

Advertising is a popular career choice so it's a challenge to break in. Writers and artists need to develop a portfolio of their best work. This might include work from school, or as a result of summer jobs. Beginners often develop samples of ads for their portfolio. For example, if you were interested in getting a job with Leo Burnett in Chicago you might prepare a sample ad for its client, Kraft Foods.

Once your portfolio is developed, you will need to visit the creative director at the agency you're interest in. Most creative directors want to see your original work rather than copies. This can make the job-search process somewhat laborious and, obviously, you will be largely confined to agencies located where you live. Creative directors will evaluate you primarily on your portfolio rather than how you are dressed or your interviewing skills. Many writers and artists are college graduates, but a four-year degree isn't required by most agencies.

Account executives usually have a business degree in marketing, or even an MBA. There are some schools of journalism such as Northwestern's Medill School, that specialize in placing students in ad agencies. Agency recruiters will put a great emphasis on how you are dressed, what you know about their agency and your interviewing skills. They look for people who are polished, articulate and will be able to relate well with their clients.

Research the agency thoroughly before the interview and be knowledgeable about its clients. You should be reading *Adverising Age* and *Adweek*, which are the bibles of the industry. These publications will keep you up on movement of clients beween agencies, as well as other trends. The publications also run a lot of ads for agencies seeking employees.

Compensation

Initially, salaries are quite low. However, they improve once you're established. Annual salaries for creative jobs start around $18,000 to $20,000. Account executives can make a little more. Since there is a lot of raiding of employees between agencies, salaries can quickly escalate once you've made a reputation for yourself. A proven way to increase your compensation is to be lured away by a competing agency. This is part of the reason why advertising people tend to switch jobs often. Salaries in the $50,000 to $60,000 range are common for fast-trackers with five years of experience. The head creative and account person working with a key account can easily earn more than $100,000 a year.

Career path

Many writers and artists don't want to pursue a management career and simply to do what they love—creating ads. Thus, the career progression for many creatives is to work on larger and more prestigious accounts. Some creative people enjoy supervision and go on to play leadership roles in their firms. Most agency presidents come from the creative side.

An account executive's career involves working on larger accounts and supervising the activities of junior account executives. An account director might supervise the activities of 5 to 10 account executives and be responsible for the overall client relationship for a major company such as Coca-Cola or Frito Lay. The vice president of account services is responsible for multiple client relationships and the strategic direction of the agency.

Major employers: Who and where

If you're serious about a career in advertising you should consider moving to New York, Los Angeles or Chicago. Alhough good firms exist in other cities, the majority of the jobs are in one of these three cities. Top agencies for creatives inlude: Leo Burnett Company, Inc., Chiat/Day, BBDO/Blair and Wieden & Kennedy. For account executives: Leo Burnett, Saatchi & Saatchi, J. Walter Thompson, Foote, Cone & Belding, and Ogilvy & Mather. The magazine *Advertising Age* publishes an annual directory of agencies and ranks firms on their business and creative capabilities.

Resources

Some key employers

BBDO/Blair
96 College Avenue
Rochester, NY 14607
716-473-0440

Ogilvy and Mather Worldwide
2 East 48th Street
New York, NY 10017
212-237-4000

Leo Burnett Company, Inc.
35 West Wacker Street
Chicago, IL 60601
312-220-5959

Saatchi & Saatchi
375 Hudson Street
New York, NY 10014
212-704-7291

Foote, Cone & Belding
1255 Battery Street
San Francisco, CA 94111
415-398-5200

J. Walter Thompson
466 Lexington Avenue
New York, NY 10017
212-210-6993/6988

Associations

American Advertising Federation
1400 K Street NW, Ste. 1000
Washington, DC 20005
202-898-0089

Association of National Advertisers
155 East 44th Street
New York, NY 10017
212-697-5950

The Advertising Educational Foundation
666 Third Avenue
New York, NY 10017
212-986-8060

International Advertising Association
342 Madison Avenue
New York, NY 10017
212-557-1133

Publications

Advertising Age
Crain Communications, Inc.
740 North Rush Street
Chicago, IL 60611
312-649-5200

Advertising/Communication Times
121 Chestnut Street
Philadelphia, PA 19106
215-629-1666

Adweek
49 East 21st Street
New York, NY 10010
212-529-5500

Marketing and Media Decisions
Decisions Publications, Inc.
1140 Avenue of the Americas
New York, NY 10036
212-935-9860

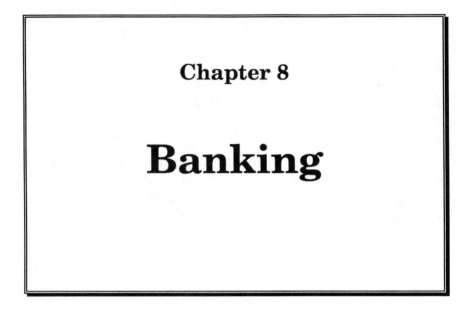

Chapter 8

Banking

Long considered a staid and stuffy profession, banking has changed dramatically. Problem loans, bank mergers and inreased foreign competition have made banking a much more dynamic and challenging career.

The primary business of a bank is to *sell money*. Ironically, money is tough to sell. The companies that banks most want to do business with are offered money left and right by other banking institutions. Since the price one bank can offer is pretty much the same as any other institution, success lies in developing the right types of relationships. Loan officers spend a lot of their time analyzing potential clients to determine which of the bank's services might benefit particular companies. These services include foreign exchange advice, import/export financing, leasing, or cash management services.

Banks are very visible in their communities and encourage their employees to become involved. Bankers often play leadership roles in the chamber of commerce and in other civic organizations. One of the activities many bankers particularly enjoy is their civic involvement

Of course, making loans is more than just sales. Lending officers must also have the necessary analytical skills to determine whether the company is deserving of the loan. George Scott, a former vice chairman of Citibank, summed it up several years ago: "I've been up and down in this business and there's still no substitute for 'What do you want the loan for? How are you going to pay me back? And what are you going to do to pay me back if your theory doesn't work out?' "

Loan officers work in a highly structured environment of checks and balances to minimize the likelihood of bad loans. If a lending officer believes a company is worthy of a loan, he or she must be adept at selling this conviction to the bank officers. This usually involves extensive presentations to convince senior bankers that the loan makes good business sense. With time, bankers develop credibility within their organizations, and while the scrutiny never disappears, it becomes less intense. The savings and loan debacle may indicate that the review process at certain institutions became far too lenient. Being a successful loan officer tests a range of skills, including analytical capabilities and the ability to develop and sustain relationships inside and outside the bank.

Some of the other areas bankers may work in include:

Retail

Typically, bankers rotate through the retail area and investigate issues such as how the bank can more effectively market itself to the consumer. They may focus on technology and how innovations such as ATM machines can be used to increase a bank's market share.

Treasury

This is the department that buys and sells money on the international market. Along with lending, this is a major profit center for many banks. This area of banking offers an environment similar to Wall Street, and tends to attract a unique breed of banker who is well-versed in international finance. An MBA is usually required to break into this function.

Where the Jobs Are

Operations

The amount of paperwork that banks generate can be overwhelming. If it is not processed accurately, the bank's ability to do business can be severely limited. Although computers carry much of the burden, operations is still labor- intensive. This area appeals to individuals who are organized and interested in management. Operations has recently received long overdue respect from the other banking areas. Since banks sell money, which is largely a commodity product, providing excellent services in the operations area is one way that a bank can differentiate itself from the competition.

What's hot and why

Banks went through a rough time in the late 1980s. Bad loans and mergers put recruiting on hold at many institutions. However, the bleak days appear to be behind the banking profession, and there is a lot of recruiting demand.

The greatest area of opportunity will be in entry-level jobs in the commercial banking and retail banking areas. More experienced bankers may find that the competition remains very intense for the few open slots. There are also some excellent opportunities with some of the Japanese banks, such as the International Bank of Japan. Japanese banks have difficulty recruiting because of anti-Japanese sentiment and a lack of Westerners in senior-level positions. They have a particular need for entry-level employees and bankers with one to three years of experience.

Breaking in

You'll need a four-year undergraduate degree in order to enter most of the training programs. Banks are pretty open-minded about your major, although you must show some quantitative capabilities. Thus, if you're an English major, make sure that you take a couple of classes in math or statistics.

Individuals without degrees can sometimes break in as tellers and then can be promoted from within. However, this is becoming increasingly rare, so it's best to invest in a four- year degree if you're serious about banking.

MBAs seem to have fallen out of favor with the commercial banks. Since banking careers tend to be highly structured, MBAs have tended to want too much too fast and weren't willing to pay their dues. Thus, a great number of banks have abandoned their MBA recruiting programs. This is good news for undergraduates, particularly liberal arts majors.

Banks look for down-to-earth, nonpretentious, smart people. Banks aren't flashy and they don't like to hire flashy people. In this regard, they are light-years away from their counterparts in investment banking on Wall Street. Since banks put a great deal of emphasis on teamwork and cooperation, make sure that, during the interview, you give examples of how you work well in groups. Banks also like to see a diversity of strengths, such as participation in athletics, and they are impressed with people who have held leadership roles in social and business organizations.

Compensation

Banks are not usually the highest-paying recruiters on campus. An annual salary for a banker hired right out of college is around $26,000. In five years, with raises and promotions, you could be earning in the mid-$30s. Six-figure salaries are usually reserved for senior vice presidents, a position that isn't usually reached until 15 to 20 years into the career.

Career path

Most bankers begin their careers in the credit training program. This in-house school covers such subjects as accounting, corporate finance, money and banking, and business law. The program lasts about one year.

Where the Jobs Are

The common joke about bankers is that virtually everyone who has worked at the bank more than a year is a vice president. Although this is an obvious overstatement, there is some truth to it. One of the reasons banks have a lot of vice presidents is that so much of a banker's activity involves calling on the business community. A prospective client is likely to feel more comfortable dealing with a vice president than he would with a senior assistant manager.

However, within banking there are vice presidents—and there are *Vice Presidents*. You can often become an assistant vice president after three years and then a full vice president in eight. The catch is that you can remain a vice president indefinitely. The first title with real teeth to it is the *senior* vice president. This individual often runs a particular department in a bank or manages a number of important client relationships. The *executive* vice presidents are the core group who actually participate in the running of the bank. They sit on the management committee and determine the strategic direction the bank will take. The executive vice president title indicates that the individual is one of the key leaders of the bank.

Major employers: Who and where

Banks exist in virtually every town in America, so you don't have to live in a major city to pursue a banking career. The powerhouses of banking are found mostly in or near New York City. They include Chemical Bank, Banker's Trust, CitiCorp and Chase Manhattan. Top banks on the West Coast include BankAmerica and Wells Fargo. First Chicago is a dominant player in the Midwest. One of the most exciting banks, with a great amount of opportunity, is NationsBank, based in North Carolina. This bank, created in 1991 through a series of mergers, has aggressive growth plans and will need capable people in order to achieve its stated objectives.

Resources

Some key employers

Banker's Trust
280 Park Avenue, 2 West
New York, NY 10017
212-850-1790

Chase Manhattan
1 Chase Manhattan Plaza,
27th Floor
New York, NY 0081
212-552-2222

Chemical Bank
225 South Street
Morristown, NJ 07960
201-539-7700

CitiCorp
399 Park Avenue
New York, NY 10043
212-559-3785

BankAmerica
Bank of America Center
555 California Street
San Francisco, CA 94104
415-953-6273

Wells Fargo
420 Montgomery
San Francisco, CA 94163
(415) 396-4561

First Chicago
1 First National Plaza
Chicago, IL 60670
312-732-4000

NationsBank
101 South Tryon
Charlotte, NC 28255
704-386-5000

Associations

**American Bankers
Association**
1120 Connecticut Ave. NW
Washington, DC 20036
202-663-5221

**Mortgage Bankers
Association of America**
1125 Fifteenth Street NW
Washington, DC 20005
202-861-6500

**National Council of
Savings Institutions**
1101 Fifteenth Street NW
Washington, DC 20005
202-857-3100

**National Association of
Bank Women, Inc.**
500 North Michigan Avenue
Chicago, IL 60611
312-661-1700

Publications

ABA Banking Journal
Simmons-Boardman
Publishing Group
345 Hudson Street
New York, NY 10014
212-620-7200

American Banker
International Thompson
Publishing Corp.
One State Street Plaza
New York, NY 10004
212-943-5280

*The Rand McNally's Bankers
Directory*
Rand McNally & Company
Financial Publishing Division
P.O. Box 7600
Chicago, IL 60680
312-673-9100

Journal of Retail Banking
Lafferty Publications
1422 West Peachtree Street
Suite 800
Atlanta, GA 30309
404-874-5120

United States Banker
Kalo Communications, Inc.
10 Valley Drive
Greenwich, CT 06831
203-869-8200

The Bankers Magazine
Warren, Gorham & Lamont
One Penn Plaza
New York, NY 10119
212-971-5000

Chapter 9

Business Consulting

Consulting may evoke a glamorous image of boardroom meetings and connections with the movers and shakers of the corporate world. While the reality is different from the image, consulting is appealing for experienced individuals who enjoy short-term projects, like working with a diversity of people, and have a large intellectual curiosity.

By most accounts, consulting is one of the fastest-growing professions. But the term covers a variety of situations. Consultants range from people working for huge multinational consulting firms to recently laid-off managers, who are continuing to provide work to former employers on a contract basis. In between are countless individuals and small firms who have carved out a niche of particular expertise.

Consulting is about advising. This is an important distinction since it accounts for one of the major frustrations consultants confront. Good consultants care passionately about their work and are devoted to assisting their clients. However, once the recommendation is made by the consultant, the responsibility for implementing the recommendation falls to in-house

71

employees. The frustrations that result are a typical reason consultants often decide to go back to work for companies.

Nevertheless, consulting has its rewards. It allows you to focus on a subject in which you have a specific interest. The project nature of the work ensures that you will not be bored. Assignments range in length from a few weeks to a year or longer. Your long-term success depends on your ability to obtain repeat assignments from clients and identify new areas in which to contribute. Thus, you must not only be an effective technician, you must also have a marketer's instinct in order to identify new opportunities.

What do consultants like most about their jobs and what are the career frustrations? The enjoyment comes from the variety of work. No two assignments are precisely alike. Consultants focus on fields in which they have expertise and in which they are particularly interested. They are often described as being "an inch wide and mile deep."

Another source of satisfaction is the project aspect of the job. Each assignment has a distinct beginning and end, which allows for a sense of closure often missing in corporate jobs. Many senior consultants also enjoy the marketing and client development process. This includes developing new consulting services and participating in sales proposals.

A major drawback is the amount of travel likely to be involved, since most of your work occurs at the client's location. While the amount of travel will vary, a majority of consultants travel 40 percent of the time. Individuals located in major metropolitan cities, such as New York, Chicago or Los Angeles, may travel less since there are more clients located nearby. Some consultants, such as financial advisers, travel less because a lot of their work is done on computers.

What's hot and why

Consulting became a hot area in the 1980s and is likely to remain energetic through the 1990s. Its growth is a result of fundamental changes in corporate America. Companies have a strong desire to reduce their fixed expenses. The largest single category of expense for a company is its people. Companies discovered that it made little sense to keep high-salaried experts on staff when there was only a periodic need for their services. Thus, the 1980s saw many individuals move from the corporate side to consulting firms as companies "outsourced" many of the functions they had performed internally.

Systems and health care are the two fields with the greatest amount of growth. Systems consultants work with the data processing departments of companies, advising them on how to make computer systems work more effectively. As the health care industry finds itself under increased pressure to manage itself as a business, consultants are providing expertise on operational, financial and marketing issues.

Breaking in

Consultants sell their expertise. Thus, this is usually not a field for the recent college graduate, although there is a lot of recruiting at the MBA level. The majority of consultants are seasoned professionals in their particular industries.

Consultants work for large firms and boutique agencies. If you have only modest experience, you might benefit from the training provided by larger firms. A company such as Andersen Consulting is unique in that it hires people directly from college and provides extensive training.

The importance of good client communications is why few consulting firms recruit people with little or no experience. Establishing credibility with a seasoned line manager can be a very difficult task for someone in his or her early 20s. The entry-level hiring profile for McKinsey, a general management consulting firm, is more typical. It seeks individuals with three to six years of experience followed by two years in an MBA program. Its typical beginning consultant may be close to 30. Consulting is a popular second career for many people.

The field places great emphasis on advanced degrees and experience. Most consultants hold a master's degree, with the MBA the most common. Technical consultants often hold a variety of Ph.D.'s.

Compensation

Since the lifestyle demands on consultants are great, they're paid well. Entry-level salaries begin in the low $30s at a firm such as Andersen Consulting, and approach $70,000 at large general management firms such as The Boston Consultng Group, and Booz, Allen & Hamilton, Inc. After five years, anual compensation runs between $45,000 and $110,000. Parters in large firms can earn in the mid six- figure range.

Career path

Consulting firms are usually structured as partnerships. The organizational structure is flat with two groups of "people-partners" and associates. Many firms have an "up or out policy" in which individuals who are unlikely to become partners are encouraged to leave.

The early years in a consulting firm are spent developing technical expertise and learning the art of becoming a consultant. Later on, more time is spent identifying new business opportunities with existing clients and selling the firm's services to new clients. Successfully marketing the firm's services and obtaining clients is critical for long-term career success. In most firms, it is impossible to become a partner if you haven't demonstrated client development skills.

Marketing and selling are the primary skills that separate partners from non-partners. Many fledgling consultants underestimate the importance of marketing and client development. If you want to provide technical consulting services and avoid selling, you may be disappointed when your career levels out early.

Major employers: Who and where

Consultants work in all the major cities in America although there are concentrations of firms in New York, Chicago and Los Angeles. If you're interested in investigating a career in consulting, the firms are easy to find. Every large public or university library has a consulting firm directory that arranges the firms by location and areas of specialization. Many individuals begin their consulting careers as independent contractors for established firms. This allows them to test consulting before committing to a full-time job.

Some of the top firms in particular fields include the following: A.T. Kearney, Inc. (production and manufacturing), American Management Systems, Inc. (information technology), Andersen Consulting (information technology), Bain & Co. (strategy), Booz, Allen & Hamilton, Inc. (general management), The Boston Consulting Group (strategy), CAP Gemini America, Inc. (information systems), Cresap (strategy), Harbridge House (human resources), Hay Group (human re-sources), Kurt Salmon (health care and retail), McKinsey & Co. (general management) and TPF&C (human resources).

Resources

Some key employers

A.T. Kearney, Inc.
222 South Riverside Plaza
Chicago, IL 60606
312-648-0111

**American Management
Systems, Inc.**
1777 North Kent Street
Arlington, VA 22209
703-841-6000

Booz, Allen & Hamilton, Inc.
101 Park Avenue
New York, NY 10178
212-697-1900

Cap Gemini America, Inc.
1133 Avenue of the Americas
New York, NY 10036
212-221-7270

Cresap
245 Park Avenue
New York. NY 10167
212-953-7000

Andersen Consulting
69 West Washington Street
Chicago, Il 60602
312-580-0069

Associations

**Professional and Technical
Consultants Association**
1330 Bascom Ave., Suite D
San Jose, CA 95128
408-287-8703

**American Association of
Professional Consultants**
9140 Ward Parkway
Kansas City, MO 64114
816-444-3500

**American Consultants
League**
1290 Palm Avenue
Sarasota, FL 34236
813-952-9290

Consultants Network
57 West 89th Street
New York, NY 10024
212-799-5239

Publications

Journal of Management Consulting
Association of Managing
Consultants
230 Park Avenue, 5th Floor
New York, NY 10169
212-697-8262

The Consultant's Voice
9140 Ward Parkway
Kansas City, MO 64114
816-444-3500

Consulting Intelligence
American Consultants League
1290 Palm Avenue
Sarasota, FL 34236
813-952-9290

The Consultants Journal
9140 Ward Parkway
Kansas City, MO 64114
816-444-3500

Chapter 10

Computers

The growth of computers and their importance in our lives cannot be underestimated. Even those of us who do not understand computers rely on them to control many functions in our cars, homes and offices. As the computer revolution continues, the employment opportunities will also expand.

What is amazing is the speed in which the computer industry has grown. For example, in 1960 there were less than 10,000 computers in existence. These machines often filled up an entire room, and by today's standards were slow in operation. The costs of owning a computer were prohibitively expensive and limited to the largest corporations. Prices began in the $100,000 range and quickly went up. In the early days, the computer market was limited to universities and large companies. Computer manufacturers such as IBM, Digital Equipment and Control Data focused their resources on serving these clients. Manufacturing computers for individuals or small business use wasn't perceived as a viable business prospect.

That all changed in 1977 when Apple Computer marketed a compact computer specifically designed for the home user. This revolutionized the nature of the computer market and heralded the computer age. Today there are more than 24 million computers in use, and some analysts predict that Americans will own 125 million computers by the year 2000. Applications for computers continue to grow as the size of the physical computer shrinks. The room-sized mainframes of the 1960s are replaced today by palm-sized notebooks capable of reading handwriting. Uses for computers are limited only by the creativity of people working with them.

The computer industry is sometimes difficult to fathom because of the language used to describe computers. Basically the entire computer industry breaks down into three major segments: hardware, software and peripherals. Computer companies focus their activities on one of these three areas.

Hardware refers to the physical machine. Computers come in a wide variety of shapes and sizes, which are becoming progressively more powerful. The very first computers that were built in the 1940s performed only a few mathematical calculations a minute. By contrast, IBM introduced in 1984 a machine that could perform 100 million multiplications per second.

Computers also come in a variety of sizes. At the top end are Supercomputers and Mainframes. Supercomputers are primarily used by the government and a few large banks. Mainframes are used as a central computing resource to provide services to remote locations. While mainframes are increasingly being replaced by smaller computers, they are still valued as an important resource by large corporations and university research centers. IBM is the industry leader in the manufacturing of mainframe computers.

Minicomputers and microcomputers are quickly replacing mainframes as the office computer of choice. These machines, which can easily fit on a desk, can often be "linked" together so that the machines can talk with each other and share information. Many companies find that microcomputers best meet their business needs.

The major area of growth in computer hardware is in the category of portable computers. Machines that can fit into briefcases are quickly becoming a common sight. Although these machines are small, many of them boast the same level of power as the desktop machines of a few years ago. Scientists at Hewlett-Packard's personal computer group estimate that the sales growth of portable computers will continue to expand at an annual clip of 60 to 80 percent. Computer hardware manufacturing is becoming a commodity business. Innovations in the design of computers are quickly copied by competitors. Thus, the hardware segment of the computer industry is increasingly focused on how computers can be manufactured quickly at the lowest possible cost.

Software is the second key area in the computer industry. If hardware is the *body* of the computer, software is the *brains*. Silicone microchips tell the machine what to do. Software enables the computer to perform tasks or applications. The software industry continues to expand as new applications for computers are created.

Finally, peripherals are the attachments that extend the range of computer usefulness. Examples include printers, modems and fax machines. By combining software and peripherals, the capabilities of computers become virtually limitless. The blending of these three components enables a wide variety of individual businesses to speed and sort data, calculate numbers and provide information to management.

The outlook continues to be bright for the computer industry. U.S. Department of Labor statistics show that more than 1 million people work directly with computers and another 2 million are employed in related fields. In the 1990s, the Bureau of Labor Statistics estimates that 725,000 new jobs will be created in the computer industry. These include: 350,000 new computer operator jobs; 150,000 new computer programmer jobs; 150,000 new computer systems analyst jobs; and 75,000 new computer technician jobs. The BLS also reports that of the five fastest-growing fields, four are in computers.

What's hot and why

The entire computer field is hot since computers are becoming more and more a part of our daily lives. Some of the jobs forecasted to be in the greatest demand are the following:

Computer operator. Operators are responsible for working with the computer hardware and the peripherals, which enable the computer to perform its designated task. Operators connect the various components in the computer's system and often troubleshoot problems when they occur. Operators begin as trainees and generally learn on the job under the guidance of an experienced operator. Most operators work in a manufacturing environment. Since many computer operations run 24 hours a day, you may be required to work rotating shifts . The job is a good starting point to break into computers.

Engineering and science technician. This title refers to a broad category of technicians who work in the computer field. They develop new products and oversee the production or manufacturing process. They may work with sophisticated testing equipment, create drawings and sketches of new products or write specifications and technical manuals.

Computer programmer. The computer programmer's job is at the core of the computer industry. The programmer uses computer language to design software programs that tell the computer what to do. Programmers use special languages such as FORTRAN and Pascal to enable the user to perform accounting functions or play interactive games. Despite the frustrations associated with writing computer programs, the final product can give you an enormous sense of satisfaction.

Computer systems analyst. This is a large and critical function within the computer industry and accounts for more than 250,000 jobs. Analysts provide expert advice on how a particular computer system can best meet the business needs of a specific company. A systems analyst understands programming and knows exactly what tasks the computer is capable of performing. Analysts are often asked to recommend the type of computer or software a company should purchase. Thus, the analyst must have a broad perspective on current computer technology, in addition to understanding the business needs of the client.

Computer engineer. Engineers research computer hardware, test new systems and work on designing such things as integrated circuits. They are often specialists on the materials used in computer manufacturing such as ceramics, silicon, plastics and metals. Other engineers are experts in lasers, optics and other electronic components. They develop cost estimates for the production of computers, and budgets and strategies for research and development initiatives. These jobs require the ability to read schematics and blueprints and demand a high level of proficiency in mathematics. Engineers typically work as a part of a small group, tackling a particular component in the design or manufacturing process.

Data processing manager. Finally, there are a number of exciting careers for individuals interested in managing a company's computing department. The data processing manager may be responsible for hundreds of employees and a large number of computer systems. In many of the large Fortune 500 corporations, the chief information officer is a critically important position and he or she often reports to the chief executive officer. The job requires sophisticated skills in managing people, equipment and budgets.

Breaking in

Two of the attractive aspects of the computer business are that people enter it at varying stages of their careers, and the educational requirements are flexible. You'll probably have to apply directly to the company in which you're interested, since campus recruiting is limited. Hiring is continual, with good jobs opening up throughout the year.

While you can obtain a computer operator or technician job with a high school degree, most people invest in an additional one- or two-year technical degree. Programmers have a four-year degree, often in computer science or mathematics. A four-year degree is required of analysts and data processing managers, with the MBA degree becoming increasingly common. Engineers usually have an undergraduate degree in chemical, mechanical, electronics or electrical engineering. Most engineers complete graduate work in their area of specialization.

Recruiters in the computer industry look for people who can function in an environment characterized by change. Skills such as adaptability and initiative are highly valued. Many computer companies use non-traditional methods of interviewing in order to evaluate the job candidate. Don't be surprised if you are asked about your philosophy of life or how you keep your internal gyroscope balanced!

Other companies, particularly in the software business, will evaluate you on your creative intelligence. For example, Micro-Soft is famous for asking individuals brainteasers such as, "Why are manhole covers round?", or, "How much does an airplane weigh?" There's no real way to prepare for the questions, so relax and try not to let the question throw you. A lot of the computer companies are small so your fit with the organization is important. If you don't get an offer because of "fit," the company is probably doing you a favor.

Compensation

Entry-level annual salary for a computer operator is from $12,000 to $15,000 a year. After five years of experience you should be earning in the $18,000 to $25,000 range. Most computer operator jobs top off at $35,000, unless you have an interest in supervision. Pursuing a management route can increase your earnings into the high $30,000 range.

Technicians begin at $20,000 to $23,000 and can progress to $48,000. Programmers begin at $24,000 to $26,000 and are usually earning $35,000 to $38,000 after five years. Many programmers who work on specialized technical problems or popular consumer programs earn more than $50,000.

Analysts with bachelor's degrees start at $24,000 to $26,000, while those with master's degrees begin at $32,000 to $35,000. An analyst with five years of experience commands a salary in the low to mid $40,000 range. Engineers command starting salaries of up to $35,000. After gaining experience, you can earn $45,000 to $60,000. If you elect to go into management, you can earn considerably more. Data processing managers often come out of the ranks of programmers or analysts and start their management careers earning between $38,000 and $42,000. The head of computers for a large corporation can earn over $100,000.

Where the Jobs Are

The key to compensation for many employees in the computer industry is stock options. This is especially true for smaller companies, which may not be able to pay the competitive salaries offered by the larger, more established companies. Stock options offer you the opportunity to purchase a specified number of shares at a predetermined price.

Career path

Career paths for individuals in the computer industry are less linear than in other fields. People drop out of the field, move back and forth between consulting and corporations, or often take time off to start their own companies. There is less predictability as to where you will wind up, which also means that there is more opportunity.

The career path of computer operators, technicians, engineers and programmers is usually from individual contributor to management. Although many individuals remain operators or programmers, supervising others offers you the chance to diversify your background and earn more money.

Most analysts begin their careers in consulting firms, then progress to supervise the work of others and to work on increasingly larger segments of a client's project. Analysts in consulting firms strive to become partners. This can usually be accomplished in 6 to 10 years, depending on the size of the firm. However, many analysts eventually decide to work for one of their clients. You may work as an internal analyst for a company and then move into supervision as a data processing manager. Then you may progress from managing the computer operations of one division to running the information systems area for an entire organization.

Major employers: Who and where

The growth of the computer industry has made it one of the more flexible careers. Although opportunities in computers exist all across the country, a large number of computer

84

companies are located outside Boston, Mass., or in Silicon Valley, Calif. New centers for computer activity have sprung up in Seattle Wash., Atlanta, Ga., and Dallas, Texas. Narrowing your choices is sometimes difficult since computers are all around you. If you're thinking about a career in computers, you might consider the following:

Companies that manufacture or sell computer hardware and software. These include well-known companies such as IBM, Apple Computer, Hewlett-Packard and Digital Equipment, along with smaller companies, a list that seems to grow weekly.

Companies and organizations that use computers. If you are interested in computer research, some of the most exciting places are the universities. Additionally, banks, retail stores and industrial companies are becoming major employers of computer professionals.

Federal, state and local government. Every federal department needs computer specialists. Government agencies are under pressure to increase the effectiveness and efficiencies of their operations. This will be accomplished through the increased use of computers, making the government an excellent job source.

Software development firms are the leading employers of computer program writers. These companies range from small startup firms with a specialized niche, to huge corporations such as MicroSoft. Software sales continue to grow at a dramatic rate. From 1984 to 1990, sales grew from $12.8 billion to $45 billion. Many software companies allow their programmers to invest in the company, which can result in substantial financial rewards.

As computers become more sophisticated, businesses increasingly need help in selecting the right computer system. Opportunities abound both in large consulting firms such as Andersen Consulting and CAP Gemini, and for independent consultants. Computer security—designing safeguards to prevent the theft of information—has recently become a hot area in the computer consulting field. Finally, as computers break down and require servicing, there is a need for service technicians and repair experts.

Resources

Some key employers

Andersen Consulting
69 West Washington Street
Chicago, IL 60602
312-580-0069

Cap Gemini America, Inc.
1133 Ave. of the Americas
New York, NY 10036
212-221-7270

Apple Computer
20525 Mariani Avenue
Cupertino, CA 95014
408-996-1010

Digital Equipment Corp.
111 Powdermill Road
Maynard, MA 01754
508-493-5111

International Business Machines Corporation
Old Orchard Road
Armonk, NY 10504
914-765-1900

Hewlett-Packard Company
3000 Hanover Street
Palo Alto, CA 94304
415-857-1501

Associations

Association of Computer Professionals
230 Park Ave., Suite 460
New York, NY 10169
212-599-3019

Association for Computer Operations Management
742 East Chapman Avenue
Orange, CA 92666
714-997-7966

Association for Women in Computing
P.O. Box 21100
St. Paul, MN 55123
612-681-9371

National Systems Programmers Association
4811 South 76th Street
Milwaukee, WI, 53220
414-423-2420

Publications

Computer
IEEE Computer Society
P.O. Box 3014
Los Alamitos, CA 90720

ComputerWorld
CW Publishing Company
P.O. Box 9171
375 Cochituate Road
Framingham, MA 01701
800-343-6474

Computer Systems News
600 Community Drive
Manhasset, NY 11030
516-562-5000

Computer Times
50 Essex Street
Rochelle Park, NJ 07662
201-843-0550

Chapter 11

Education

The American educational system offers jobs in teaching and administration at primary, secondary and university levels. Although few people get rich in education, satisfaction comes from positively influencing young people.

Universities are finding themselves facing a shortage of capable teachers in such fields as computers and marketing. Although it is virtually impossible to become a tenured professor without a Ph.D., an increasing number of colleges are actively recruiting adjunct or part-time teachers who have bachelor's degrees and extensive experience in these fields. Colleges and universities have found that experienced professionals in many different areas bring a real-world perspective to the classroom, and this is greatly appreciated by the students.

It is the intangible rewards that attract most people to teaching. The satisfaction that comes from working for more than just a paycheck is one the prime reasons why individuals decide to enter education. The predictability of the academic calendar and the possibility of "summer vacations" are other draws to education.

People in education often comment about how much they enjoy working in a school setting. Going to work each day on a campus is a unique experience. Educational institutions take great pride in maintaining an environment that encourages the freedom of expression. This results in a vibrant culture in which to work. It's also interesting to work at a place in which the age of the students, with whom you interact on a day-to-day basis, stays constant. Long-term academics sometimes realize that while they have aged, their surroundings have not. Living in a perpetual time warp, while somewhat unreal, can be enjoyable.

What's hot and why

There are three main areas of opportunity. As the mini-baby boom generation continues to age, a shortage of elementary and secondary schoolteachers is already noticeable. This is especially true in smaller towns. Secondly, the competition among schools to recruit top Ph.D.'s will remain intense. And finally, opportunities for development directors, who head up the fund-raising activities for educational institutions, are plentiful.

More than 700,000 people are employed by the faculties of our nation's colleges. The role of the faculty member is characterized by three elements: teaching, research and service. Of the three, research is the most important in order to obtain the coveted status of tenured professor.

Tenure is basically a commitment from the university to provide the professor with lifetime employment. Its original purpose was to safeguard teachers with controversial opinions from being censured or fired by others on the faculty. A "tenure track" professor has five years to become tenured. Although feedback is provided along the way, the decision is still a major event and often a surprise. Achieving tenure offers status and security. It is largely determined by how many papers the faculty member has published and the status of the publications. Once tenured status has been obtained, you are free to continue to do research, consult or focus on teaching. It gives you freedom unmatched in any other profession.

Some faculty members decide not to be considered for tenure. They work on one- to three-year contracts and may work for more than one educational institution at a time. This path is best if you want to focus on teaching. By lecturing at a number of different schools and on different subjects, you'll have a career that offers a great amount of independence and variety. Since there are ongoing needs for adjunct professors and lecturers, once you have established your reputation, the work is usually quite plentiful.

Elementary and secondary schoolteachers are the backbone of the educational system. The shortage of these teachers is expected to become worse in the 1990s. More than 1.6 million people work as elementary schoolteachers, and another 1.2 million teach in our high schools. Most elementary and secondary teachers work a nine-month year with summers off.

The hottest administrative field is development. The development officer is responsible for bringing in money to support the college or school within a university. The development officer identifies prospective donors not only by their net worth, but also by their interests. What can be offered that might motivate them to give money to the school? Are they alumni? Have they mentioned in speeches the importance of education? Do they need a tax break? Can the development officer appeal to their ego? For $1 million, a school might name a professorship for a contributor. For $5 million, the school might be named for the donor!

The development officer works on putting together the fund-raising strategy. The wooing process can take several years. The development officer is in a highly visible role since the financial demands of educational institutions are great.

Breaking in

In order to be a college professor you'll need a Ph.D. for most jobs. Although you can be hired as an adjunct professor or lecturer with a bachelor's degree and significant work experience, you'll need the Ph.D. to achieve tenure.

Each year there are meetings that serve to introduce the new Ph.D.'s to the schools that have openings. Openings are widely publicized, and the meetings serve as the initial step in the recruiting process. There is a pecking order among schools, based on their reputations in a particular field of study. No one school is excellent in everything. For example, Harvard would be a top choice for a prospective faculty member specializing in English literature. However, the school would have little appeal for a Ph.D. specializing in engineering.

You'll be hired largely on the quality of your research, the reputation of the school you graduated from and your references. You may be asked to make a presentation on your research to members of the faculty. Although teaching is a large part of every young faculty member's life, interpersonal skills aren't usually a major factor in the selection decision.

Jobs for experienced professors are usually advertised in the trade paper, *The Chronicle of Higher Education*. Word of mouth also plays a pivotal role in finding jobs. The executive recruiting firms, thus far, don't do much work in this area.

Elementary and secondary schoolteachers need a bachelor's degree from an approved teacher training program. As a part of obtaining your degree you will work as a student teacher, which gives you a first-hand look at what teaching is like. Many states require their teachers to have graduate degrees.

Interviews are usually conducted in the late spring or early summer to replace teachers who are leaving. You may interview with a selection committee consisting of other teachers and the school principal. In addition to your educational background, you should be prepared for questions such as:

"What attracted you to teaching?"

"What gives you the greatest amount of satisfaction about teaching?"

"Do you think you can handle the frustrations of teaching?"

The panel will assess you on your ability to work well with children or teenagers. An ideal candidate will impress the panel with his or her ability to inspire students to develop a love for learning. You also may be asked about your willingness to participate in extracurricular activities, such as directing a school play or coaching an athletic team.

Jobs for development directors usually require an undergraduate degree but exceptions are sometimes made for people with extensive experience in the field. Interviewers look for individuals who are creative, assertive and present a highly polished image. Since development directors spend their time calling on senior-level corporate executives and wealthy individuals, you need to have a great amount of poise and excellent interpersonal skills. Many development directors are well-connected socially, which is a benefit in raising money.

Openings are regularly advertised in *The Chronicle of Higher Education* or are posted on a bulletin board outside of the university's personnel office.

Compensation

For college-level teachers, the salary range is quite wide depending upon the school and area of specialization. As a general rule, private schools pay higher than public schools. Professors in the fields of medicine, law, engineering and business are paid the most. Assistant professors coming right out of doctoral programs earn $25,000 to $60,000 for nine months, associate professors earn $30,000 to $70,000, and full professors command $50,000 to $90,000. If you have the good fortune to receive a "chaired" professorship, salaries of $100,000 are possible. Many professors supplement their teaching salaries with consulting work, which can increase total compensation by up to 50 percent.

Entry-level salaries for elementary and secondary school-teachers range from $14,000 to $20,000. Teachers with five years of experience average $21,000 to $35,000. Salaries top off at $45,000 to $50,000 but can be supplemented by summer work.

Development assignments start at $25,000 to $30,000. A development manager with five to eight years of experience can command $38,000 to $45,000. The development director for a large institution can earn $75,000 to $95,000. Average annual increases for all education positions are running from 3 percent to 6 percent.

Career path

Once tenure is achieved, many professors teach, conduct research and do consulting work. Some professors are attracted to the management issues involved in running a school, and they become administrators. A professor might become department chairman after 10 to 15 years, then an associate dean and, finally, dean of the school. A dean's job usually requires 20 years of experience. The top jobs in a university—president, chancellor and provost—are usually held by professors with 25 to 30 years of experience.

Sometimes, elementary and secondary schoolteachers go into administration. However, since there are less administrative slots, it's more difficult to do. Moreover, teachers are generally drawn to the profession because of their love of teaching. If some leave the profession, they can use many of their skills in the human resources departments of large corporations.

Development officers usually begin their careers as the second- or third-level person in a development office. It is common for development officers to move from institution to institution in order to progress. A development officer might work for a university, a nonprofit organization, a museum and then back to a university, all in the course of a career. After 10 to 12 years, a development officer can be running the function for a school within the university. The top development job, supervising the activities of 8 to 15 development officers, is usually obtained 15 to 20 years into the career.

Major employers: Who and where

Education opportunities exist in every town. Professors usually choose a college or university because of its location or reputation. Elementary and secondary schoolteachers can find out about opportunities in their area from the superintendent of schools or the state department of education. The National Education Association in Washington, D.C., may also be of assistance.

Development opportunities are usually listed in either your local paper or in *The Chronicle of Higher Education*. You may also wish to apply directly to schools in your area. Check your yellow pages for a listing of educational institutions.

A good source for listings and descriptions of all two- and four-year colleges is *Lovejoy's College Guide*, edited by Charles T. Straughn II and Barbara Lovejoy Straughn (Prentice Hall, 1991).

Resources

Associations

National Education Association
1201 Sixteenth Street NW
Washington, DC 20036-
202-822-7200

National School Boards Association
1680 Duke Street
Alexandria, VA 22314
703-838-6722

American Federation of Teachers
555 New Jersey Ave. NW
Washington, DC 20001
202-879-4400

National Association for Women in Education
1325 18th Street NW
Washington, DC 20036
202-659-9330

Publications

NEA Today
National Education Assoc.
1201 Sixteenth Street NW
Washington, DC 20036-3290
202-822-7200

The Chronicle of Higher Education
1255 23rd Street NW,
Washington, DC 20037
202-466-1000

American Teacher
555 New Jersey Avenue
Washington, DC 20002
202-879-4400

The Education Digest
416 Longshore Drive
Ann Arbor, MI 48105
313-769-1211

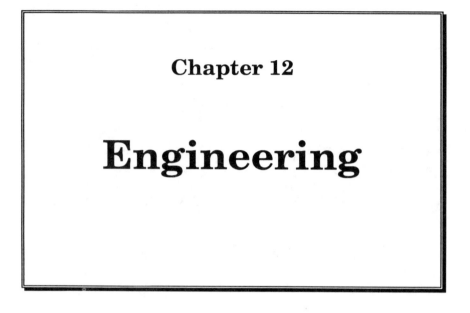

Chapter 12

Engineering

Although college recruitment has recently hit an all-time low, engineering students continue to find themselves in great demand, with starting salaries approaching $35,000. Engineering encompasses a variety of disciplines, and addresses problems as diverse as reducing pollution levels, designing more powerful computers and extracting oil from porous rock. Engineering requires knowledge about the theories of science, in addition to practical expertise, in order to find solutions to technical problems.

Engineering is a field of specialization. New fields such as biomedical engineering are becoming very attractive to students. Many engineers develop, within their areas, a subspecialty that may draw from a variety of different disciplines. For example, ceramic engineers often have backgrounds encompassing chemistry, and chemical and mechanical engineering.

While most engineers are drawn to the profession out of their desire to work on specific problems, engineers who work for large manufacturing companies often pursue careers in administration, management or sales.

What's hot and why

Engineering has been one of the most consistently hot fields in the past decade and it doesn't appear to be cooling off. The reason is twofold: First, our colleges and universities don't produce enough engineers Engineering is a demanding discipline of study, requiring strengths in both science and math. However, if you have an aptitude in these areas and are willing to work hard in school, the field is packed with opportunities.

Secondly, engineering is about the future. Engineers are working on new methods to keep us healthy, heat our homes and produce food. Almost every innovation requires engineering input. The demand for engineers is far greater than the supply.

Let's take a look at where the hot jobs are:

Biomedical engineers. This concentration applies engineering principles to solve medical or health-related problems. This is a new field that has grown extensively in the past five years. As the population continues to age, biomedical engineering is almost certain to remain one of the hot fields in engineering.

Biomedical engineers created the pacemaker and are now working on the development of artificial hearts and kidneys. Other biomedical engineers specialize in medical equipment, such as new applications for surgical lasers. Still others specialize in systems to increase the efficiency of laboratories, hospitals and clinics.

Biomedical engineers work in teams with other professionals, including scientists, chemists and physicians. Many work at universities that are affiliated with hospitals or medical complexes.

Chemical engineers. Chemical engineering is a highly complex and specialized field that investigates how chemicals can be used for research and manufacturing. Chemical engineers have been involved in the introduction of many products we now take for granted, such as nylon, rayon and other synthetic fabrics. They also design torpedoes, cigarette filters and emission control systems.

Where the Jobs Are

Many chemical engineers are employed by chemical, oil refining or plastics industries. Given the diverse problems on which chemical engineers work, the area is expected to continue growing during the 1990s. Recently, chemical engineers have become involved in environmental protection issues.

Electrical engineers. These professionals works on the design and production of electrical and electronic equipment, including radar equipment, microwave transmission systems and stereo systems. The growth of the computer industry is one of the major reasons for the increased demand for electrical engineers. The engineering function plays a critical role in enabling companies to develop more powerful, smaller computers. As computer manufacturers are increasingly confronted with issues associated with manufacturing machines, electrical engineers will continue to be in demand in this area.

Electrical engineering is the largest engineering discipline. As the computer and communications industries continue to grow, the demand for electrical engineers is expected to follow along parallel lines.

Industrial engineers. Industrial engineering is a unique segment of engineering, focusing primarily on productivity. Industrial engineers examine how workers in manufacturing plants can become more productive. For example, an industrial engineer will investigate the ideal location for a company to set up a manufacturing facility. Factors such as taxes, the education level of the work force, and proximity to transportation centers are part of the analysis. Once the site has been selected, the industrial engineer will recommend, based on the anticipated work flow, how the machinery inside the plant should be arranged.

One of the most challenging and often controversial roles of the industrial engineer concerns worker productivity. The industrial engineer observes people on their jobs with the goal of increasing efficiency. He or she examines the precise steps workers take in performing their jobs to determine if a particular step can be eliminated. Since these recommendations sometimes result in the cutting of jobs, the presence of an industrial engineer at the manufacturing site is often not welcomed by the line workers. However, as American businesses wrestle with the complex task of increasing worker productivity, the role of the industrial engineer will be in demand.

Mechanical engineers. These are the inventors in the engineering world. Mechanical engineers hold the largest number of patents, and have invented thousands of mechanical devices. They work on everything from rocket engines to refrigerators to elevators. Mechanical engineering is one of the broadest fields within engineering.

Since this specialty is so broad, mechanical engineers specialize in a particular area. It might be automotive, energy, heating, ventilating or air conditioning. They are often involved in the design of custom machinery for companies who manufacture a wide array of products.

Job growth in this area is projected to continue through the 1990s. As machinery becomes more complex and multiple steps in the manufacturing process are conducted by a single machine, the demand for mechanical engineers will increase.

The outlook for engineering is very bright. Technological advances and a competitive international market have placed a renewed emphasis on manufacturing and innovation.

Breaking in

An undergraduate degree in engineering is required for virtually any entry-level position. Many engineers go on to pursue a master's degree in order to learn a new technology. For example, nuclear engineering is taught mostly at the graduate level. An advanced degree is also helpful for promotion purposes, and a master's is required for most teaching positions. The MBA degree is helpful to increase your understanding of practical business issues. This is important to many engineering disciplines, such as industrial and chemical engineering.

Engineers should have a strong interest and aptitude for math and science. Since engineers work both by themselves and in groups, you should feel comfortable doing both. Communication skills are also important, particularly for industrial engineers who interact with more people than workers in other branches of engineering.

Where the Jobs Are

A great amount of entry-level recruiting is done on college campuses. Since engineers are in demand, companies make it easy for students to find out about job opportunities. Job openings are well-publicized through placement offices. Companies also contact professors for their recommendations. Thus, it's a good idea to make sure your professors know where your career interests lie. Take the extra step of giving your professor a copy of your resume. The more they know about you, the better they are at selling you to a recruiter.

The on-campus interview is usually conducted by either an engineer from the company or a representative from the human resources department. Engineers often have difficulty with the human resources interviewers, who don't speak the engineering language. This interviewer places an emphasis on interpersonal skills. Before the interview, ask your placement director if he or she knows who will be coming on campus to interview. If a human resources manager will be doing the interview, invest some time working on your interviewing skills. Many placement offices allow you the chance to do a video-taped "mock" interview. This is very helpful in letting you see how others see you.

The interviewers will also ask you about grades and what you learned in a relevant class. Be specific if this question comes up.

Experienced engineers, those with a specific technical expertise or extensive management capabilities, find their jobs through executive recruiters specializing in engineers, or help-wanted ads. Advertisements that appear in the back of engineering trade journals are a particularly good source of job opportunity information.

Compensation

Entry-level salaries are approaching $35,000 for college graduates. Some Ph.D. graduates have commanded $50,000 to $60,000. Biomedical, chemical and electrical engineers are commanding the highest salaries, while industrial engineers earn the least.

Entry-level salaries have dramatically escalated in recent years, placing pressure on internal salary levels. Often an experienced engineer makes only a few thousand dollars more than a recent graduate. This "internal salary compression" issue is a major problem for companies that recruit a lot of engineers. Five to eight years into the career, compensation is usually in the $45,000 to $55,000 range. Laboratory engineers top out around $80,000. Engineers who pursue a management track can earn considerably more. A corporate vice president of engineering can make more than $150,000 at a technically oriented company.

Another source of compensation, particularly for engineers working in the high technology industry, are stock options. Often granted by smaller organizations in lieu of large paychecks, these options can make their holders wealthy if the company does well. Many electrical engineers in Silicon Valley have made substantial sums of money in this manner.

Career path

As often seen in technical careers, the career path is either into management or into more specialized areas of research. Most engineers who initially work for a corporation eventually pursue a management career path. The first three to five years are typically spent working in research before the individual is offered the opportunity to supervise others. The first management assignment is often as a project leader, supervising the work of three to five engineers. A group manager supervises the activities of three to five project managers. A department manager is often responsible for 50 to 100 engineers and a budget of more than $1 million. The vice president of engineering is responsible for the overall management of the function. This person normally reports to the president of the company. The position usually requires 20 years of experience.

Engineers who don't wish to pursue a management career track may find consulting or academia to be more rewarding than industry. Both of these environments encourage an individual to focus on research and project work. You will normally need a Ph.D. to work at a university, and most consulting firms encourage their consultants to obtain an advanced degree.

Major employers: Who and where

Engineers typically work in four sectors of the economy. Manufacturing companies employ about 50 percent of the engineers. Manufacturers who hire large numbers of engineers include the electronics, aircraft, chemical, oil, scientific instruments, automobile and aircraft industries. Public utilities also recruit certain types of engineers. The government— particularly the departments of defense, energy and NASA—is also a large employer.

The following associations may also be of assistance in career placement. Biomedical Engineering Society, Culver City, Calif.; American Institute of Chemical Engineers, New York; Institute of Electrical & Electronics Engineers, Washington, D.C.; American Institute of Industrial Engineers, Norcross, Ga., and The American Society of Mechanical Engineers, New York.

Resources

Associations

Biomedical Engineering Society
P.O. Box 2399
Culver City, CA 90231
213-206-6443

American Institute of Chemical Engineers
345 East 47th Street
New York, NY 10017
212-705-7338

Institute of Electrical & Electronics Engineers
345 East 47th Street
New York, NY 10017
212-705-7900

American Institute of Industrial Engineers
25 Technology Park/Atlanta
Norcross, GA 30092
404-449-0460

The American Society of Mechanical Engineers
345 East 47th Street
New York, NY 10017
212-705-7722

Society of Women Engineers
345 East 47th Street
New York, NY 10017
212-705-7855

Publications

Biomedical Technology Information Service
1351 Titan Way
Brea, CA 92621
714-738-6400

Mechanical Engineering
345 East 47th Street
New York, NY 10017
212-705-7782

Chemical Engineering
1221 Ave. of the Americas
New York, NY 10020
212-512-4653/3696

Electronic Products News
One Penn Plaza, 26th Floor
New York, NY 10119
212-239-1406

Chapter 13

Entertainment

Ah, the lure of show biz! Meetings. Deals. Schmoozing with the beautiful people. No wonder the entertainment field is so popular. However, the glamour and glitz mask an extremely competitive business.

There are two general job groups: creative and business.The creative occupations include writers, actors and technicians, such as camera operators, sound technicians, set designers, best boys, grips, boom operators and swing operators. On any given day less than 5 percent of the members of SAG (the Screen Actors Guild, the union for actors) are working, and the average salary for all actors barely tops $9,000. You've got to have greasepaint in your veins to play the enormous odds against achieving acting success.

What's hot and why

Although the entertainment field is very competitive to break into, the number of jobs are, in fact, increasing. New television programs, films and music must be continually pro-uced. The advent of cable has spawned a variety of new com-anies to produce entertainment products. Overall, the total number of companies in the entertainment industry has in-reased in the past decade. While in the 1950s the major studios handled all aspects of the entertainment process internally, to-ay the industry is far more fragmented with specialized com-anies providing such services as sound recording, film editing, set design and special effects. This has made the various com-onents in the entertainment industry more visible and easier to target.

Most people identify a particular area in which they are interested and work hard to develop an expertise. Thus, the technical side of the entertainment industry is dominated by specialists rather than generalists. Once your reputation is es-tablished, word of mouth can play a major role in keeping you busy.

However, you need to be prepared for a slightly nomadic lifestyle. Most creative people work on a project-by-project bas-is with no guarantee of future employment. Moreover, as film and TV production is increasingly happening in a variety of lo-cations, you may spend considerable time away from home.

Let's take a quick look at some creative jobs that offer the best opportunities to break into the entertainment field:

Story editor. This individual is usually an employee of one of the studios and evaluates screenplays and books. A large part of the job is developing relationships with publishers and agents who submit the manuscripts. The story editor evaluates potential publications and plays a critical role in selecting the raw material that will eventually become a movie or television show.

Casting director. He or she is responsible for finding, auditioning and sometimes negotiating the services of actors and actresses. Once the script is decided, the casting director will develop a list of potential actors and actresses based on the requirements of the role. The casting director works closely with the talent agents, schedules interviews, and narrows the field to a group of finalists presented to the director for final approval.

Where the Jobs Are

Grip. The grip works for the director of photography and is responsible for the physical movement and placement of cameras, cranes, booms, etc. He or she supervises the transporting, rigging, placement and operation of all of the equipment. The assistant to the grip is called the best boy. Additional assistants to grips are called hammers, because they (surprise!) all carry hammers. These are great jobs for people who want a physically demanding technical assignment in the entertainment industry.

Negative cutter. This person works for the film editor and makes the actual cuts in the raw film footage. This is exacting precision work, since some segments are edited frame by frame. It's a job in which there's no room for mistakes because you are working with the original irreplaceable footage. Cutters generally start in the production lab as assistants and work their way up.

The second group of careers focus on the business aspects of the entertainment industry. Areas of opportunity include talent agents, publicists and distribution managers.

Unit publicist. The publicist is responsible for creating awareness about a film and building an audience. A unit publicist prepares the publicity campaign, writes promotional material about the film and sets up interviews with the cast and the media. A lot of publicists start out working for one of the public relations firms in Los Angeles and then use their specialized area of expertise in one of the studios.

Distribution executive. A distribution executive negotiates the terms by which the film will be shown in national theaters. He or she negotiates such issues as what percentage of the ticket price the theater will keep, and how long a theater will guarantee to run a film. Negotiating skills are critical for success since each deal is slightly different from the next. Distribution and publicity are highly specialized areas and individuals tend to spend their careers in these areas.

Talent agent. This is the experience you want if you have your eye on a senior-level job in the entertainment business. Most of the leaders in the industry either started their careers with a talent agency or spent some time in the field. It's the only job that gives you both a broad education and perspective on the business side of the entertainment business. It's the ultimate *hot job* in the entertainment field.

While resented in some corridors of the entertainment business, agents have carved out a niche for themselves. The agent functions as a broker between the manufacturers of the entertainment product (such as film studios and record manufacturers) and the talent (actors, singers and writers). Since each group needs the other, the agent's role in bringing them together is indispensable.

Agents live and die by the talent that they represent. Thus, it is an extremely competitive job. Agents spend considerable time courting prospective clients and ensuring that existing clients aren't listening to the siren songs of other agents.

Breaking in

So what's the best way to actually get your foot in the door? First, think about geography. It's difficult to be successful if you aren't in one of the entertainment industry's capitals— New York or Los Angeles. Conducting a job search from St. Louis is impractical so be prepared to move to one of these two cities if you're really serious about breaking into the business. Of the two cities, Los Angeles offers the greater number of opportunities, unless you are interested in working on Broadway or in live theater. As the entertainment industry continues to expand, new cities such as Atlanta, the home of Ted Turner's broadcasting empire, are also worth considering. However, most people want to be in one of the two hubs.

Networking is the key if you want to break in. Chances are that you don't have any personal friends already in the business, so the first steps are going to be the toughest. Survey all of your personal and family acquaintances to see if they have any connections, however remote. People have broken into the business because their uncle was a partner with a Cleveland public accounting firm that happened to audit one of the movie studios. Uncle made a phone call that cracked open the door.

If you don't have any personal contacts, industry experts' best advice is to save up three months of living expenses and go to New York or Los Angeles. If you literally bang on enough doors and are relentless in talking with everyone you possibly can, your odds of eventually breaking in are surprisingly good. If you're worried about offending people by being too aggressive, or aren't 100 percent committed to a career in the entertainment field, save yourself time, money and effort and pursue something else. Executives say that it's not lack of talent that trips people up, but a lack of tenacity.

In the early stages, don't reject any job as beneath you if it can open doors and teach you about the inner workings of the business. Although working in the mail room at the William Morris Agency may not appear glamorous, it is one of the most highly coveted positions. Regardless of where you start, take advantage of every opportunity to learn. Work hard to establish relationships with people who can help you.

Compensation

Studio employees in the publicity and distribution areas, and technical workers associated with production are often covered under union contracts. Annual earnings at the entry level range from $15,000 to $35,000. After five years of experience, average earnings run from $45,000 to $60,000. Pay tends to top out at $75,000 to $85,000.

A writer may sell an option on his or her first script for $10,000. If the script is eventually produced, the writer could earn another $50,000. If the subsequent script is a commercial success, the author can name his or her price. For example, "Lethal Weapon" writer Shane Black sold his next script, "The Last Boy Scout" for a record $1.75 million in 1990. That was quickly surpassed by Joe Esterhas, writer of "Flashdance" and "Jagged Edge," who sold his script for the movie "Basic Instinct" for $3 million.

Rookie agents consider themselves lucky to be offered $25,000 to $30,000 to start. Five to eight years into the career, a successful agent should have recruited an initial group of clients and be earning $75,000 to $100,000. An experienced agent, representing major entertainment talent, can earn a compensation package of over $1 million. However, your earnings are going to be directly related to the earnings of the talent you represent. Thus, an agent's earnings can fluctuate widely from year to year.

Career path

So you want to be a mogul? How do you begin? The time-honored method of future "mogulhood" has not changed over the past 30 years. When you look at the starting point of such industry heavyweights as David Geffen, Michael Ovitz or Barry Diller, the answer is the same: the mail room at the William Morris Agency. The pay is lousy and the work is often belittling. However, this well-known talent agency has traditionally been the best place to start. Beginning your career in the mail room gives you a unique perspective on how the entertainment business works. You'll learn about deals and personalities, and develop an in-depth understanding about how things really get done.

The most common route out of the mail room is by establishing a relationship with an agent and becoming his or her assistant. Although an assistant's job is often little more than secretarial in nature, it enables you to make contact with the next level of players. Since the business is so close-knit, personal relationships are critical to accomplishing anything. In the entertainment industry, the trading of favors back and forth is the coin of the realm.

Breaking out of the assistant's role is typically achieved by one of two ways. The next step depends upon what type of position you're looking for. The entertainment industry has needs for accountants, computer programmers and administrators, like any other business. Most individuals who desire a career in the entertainment business want to be in the "business of the business" which means working with the "talent."

Talent is what makes the world go 'round in the entertainent field. It comes in many forms, such as an actor, a book, a play, or a song. Successful entertainers share a common trait—

they have estabished a relationship with some component of talent. The ability to spot and identify new talent is one of the most common means by which to establish your reputation. Since the entertainment business is heavily youth-driven, young people with an eye for what's hot and in style often progress faster than they would in other businesses.

Major employers: Who and where

If you're serious about a career in the entertainment industry you've got to be in one of its capitals: New York or Los Angeles. The hot studios or film production companies include Disney, Tri-Star, Fox, Time Warner and Paramount. The top talent agency by far is Creative Artists Agency. Its roster of clients dominates the entertainment industry. Other agencies in the top tier include: William Morris, International Creative Management, and Creative Artists. Specialized companies, which provide support to the entertainment industry, are often listed in the yellow pages, or can be identified through AFTRA, the primary entertainment union.

Resources

Some key employers

The Walt Disney Company
500 South Buena Vista Street
Burbank, CA 91521
818-560-1000

Paramount Pictures Corp.
5555 Melrose Avenue
Hollywood, CA 90038
213-956-5000

Fox, Inc.
10201 Pico Boulevard
Los Angeles, CA 90035
213-277-2211

Creative Artists Agency, Inc.
9830 Wilshire Blvd.
Beverly Hills, CA 90212
310-288-4545

Time Warner, Inc.
75 Rockefeller Plaza
New York, NY 10019
212-484-8000

William Morris Agency Inc.
151 El Camino Drive
Beverly Hills, CA 90212
310-274-7451

Asssociations

Show Business Association
1501 Broadway
New York, NY 10036
212-354-7600

**Entertainment Industry
Referral and Assistance Ctr.**
11132 Ventura Boulevard,
Studio City, CA 91604
818-848-9997

**Educational Theatre
Association**
3368 Central Parkway
Cincinnati, OH 45225
513-559-1996

Association of Entertainers
P.O. Box 1393
Washington, DC 20013
202-546-1919

Publications

Back Stage
303 West 42nd Street
New York, NY 10036
212-947-0020

Variety
154 West 46th Street
New York, NY 10036
212-869-5700

Show Business
1501 Broadway, Penthouse
New York, NY 10036
212-354-7600

Amusement Business
49 Music Square West
Nashville, TN 37202
615-321-4267

Chapter 14

Finance/ Wall Street

Wall Street is more than a location. People work at "Wall Street" jobs in St. Louis, Atlanta, San Francisco and many other cities. More than anything else, Wall Street jobs are about money—making it, analyzing it and investing it. Unless you're passionate about the subject of money, you're likely to feel out of place.

What's hot and why

Wall Street jobs really refer to a variety of positions within the world of finance and investments. The industry is characterized by periods of great growth and decline. It's a world of booms and busts. For example, in the early 1980s as the bull market roared along, thousands of recently minted business students headed for Wall Street. The amount of money you could make at a tender age was staggering. MBA graduates with two to three years of experience could earn more than $100,000, and their bosses earned millions. Young people

113

Where the Jobs Are

headed to business school with the sole intent of using the degree to secure one of these golden jobs. Then the party abruptly stopped in October 1987. When the market crashed, thousands of investment professionals found themselves on the street with no clue as to what to do next. However, as we enter the mid-1990s, hiring activity is picking up.

Jobs in the investment community vary considerably in terms of ease of entry, educational requirements and day-to-day responsibilities. What all of the jobs share is the subject of money—and the chance to earn a great deal of it.

Hot jobs in finance include stockbrokers, analysts, merger experts and traders. Each of these jobs requires unique skills and is attractive to different types of people.

Most people who work in finance are stockbrokers. As the stock market expands, the recruiting of brokers increases dramatically. Working as a stockbroker is challenging and difficult, especially during the first few years. You can expect that it will take at least two years to develop a substantial client base. These clients are referred to as your book of business. While developing clients is difficult and requires endless cold calling, once you obtain a client, he or she will probably stay with you for many years. Gradually, referrals replace colds calls as the primary source of new business. With an average compensation for stockbrokers of $100,000 per year, most people feel that the early frustrations are ultimately worth the effort.

Analysts are also in demand as the financial markets continue to grow. Analysts predict which stocks are good to buy, hold or sell. They will usually specialize in a particular industry, such as high technology, utilities or pharmaceuticals. Much of their day is spent analyzing a company's financial performance, introducing new products and studying the competition's growth. They'll also look at how general economical factors affect the financial performance of the company. The job is heavily analytical and usually requires an MBA degree. While most of these positions are located in New York, analysts can also find jobs in major cities such as Los Angeles, Chicago and Atlanta. Opportunities continue to be created as existing players retire or move to competing firms.

The demand for talent in mergers and acquisitions (or M&A) is growing as the number of merging companies grows. Much of the work of the M&A specialist involves analyzing a company's financial performance in order to develop a true picture of its strengths and weaknesses. Sales ability is required to identify potential companies with which the client company can merge.

Trading has always attracted individuals who are interested in gambling for enormous stakes. As the number of stock exchanges grows, there are more opportunities for individuals to break into the field. Trading demands strong quantitative skills, aggressiveness and a very strong competitive bent. Most traders work in either New York, San Francisco or Chicago. They are recognizable to most of us as the people on the evening business news wearing the funny colored coats and waving their arms back and forth. Traders make their money on small fluctuations in the prices of various commodities. They bet on which way the price of a particular good, such as gold or pork bellies, will go. This is a true gambler's profession. Fortunes are made and lost, often by the same people, in the fast-moving commodities market.

Breaking in

Most brokerage firms look for people with a college degree, although the type of degree can vary. Some firms recruit on campus, but most stock brokerages welcome individuals who contact them directly. Many liberal arts graduates have had very successful careers as stockbrokers. Quantitative capabilities are required to pass the Series 7 exam, which is required of all brokers before they can buy or sell stocks for their clients. The firms usually provide the training and preparation for the test.

A question many people ask themselves is whether to work for a large national firm or a smaller local one. The advantage of the larger firms is the training and support they offer. Certain large firms, such as Merrill Lynch, have developed a reputation for superior training. Merrill Lynch's training program is so renowned that its employees are often recruited away by other firms.

The most important consideration in choosing a firm is the person who will be responsible for your training. While all sales managers have an incentive to make you successful, some are better at it than others. Try to find a person who has a successful track record as a broker and is committed to providing support beyond the initial trial period. The retail brokerage business, like any sales job, has its peaks and valleys. You'll want a boss who can help you manage and navigate the inevitable lows, in addition to offering you advice on how to strike when the iron is hot.

Analysts and M&A staffers are heavily recruited from MBA programs. It is quite difficult to break in without an advanced business or economics degree. Interviewers will be particularly interested in your quantitative skills. They often assess this by throwing number problems at you in the interview. Recruiters also believe that if you're serious about a job on Wall Street you should know a lot about financial current events. Thus, don't be surprised if you're asked to name the chancellor of the exchequer.

While more college graduates are drawn to trading, the field requires no specific educational degree. To become a trader you must be highly quantitative and have a "feel" for the market. A "feel" is most commonly described as a sixth sense for which way the market is going.

Trading is a business of early entry. Many traders begin quite young, often just out of high school, as runners or administrative assistants. If you want to be a trader you must be willing to live near one of the trading centers in the United States. Chicago and New York are considered the best cities, although smaller trading operations exist in a few other cities. Runners and clerks are hired on a regular basis since there is a high level of turnover. Runners carry the paper on which the traders record the transaction to the office in which the trade is processed. Progression from runner to full-time trader depends upon your convincing someone to give you a shot. Most traders start out leasing a seat on the exchange, and if they are successful, they will eventually buy their own seat. Seats currently cost more than \$150,000, although prices fluctuate greatly. Once you're started, it will be your gambling instincts, market savvy and luck that determine your ultimate success.

Compensation

As a stockbroker, your compensation depends on your productivity. The more business you do, the more money you'll make. Most firms will offer you a gradually declining base salary supplemented by commissions. Over time you should be able to generate commissions greater than your salary. Although the guaranteed salary is important for newcomers to the business, savvy players look at what percentage of the gross earnings the firms pays out. Starting salaries range from \$18,000 to \$35,000. Stockbrokers with five to eight years of exerience average \$90,000 to \$100,000. Extremely successful brokers can earn \$300,000 or more during a bull market.

Analysts and M&A professionals are compensated with starting base salaries of \$50,000 to \$60,000. This may also be supplemented by an annual bonus of 25 to 50 percent. Experienced workers typically earn a six-figure salary. Analysts normally top out at \$150,000 to \$200,000. M&A experts made millions of dollars on transactions such as the buyout of RJR/Nabisco.

A trader is the ultimate gambler, so earnings will fluctuate widely. It takes a little while to get started, so your first year's earnings are commonly in the \$20,000 range. After the initial year, you may earn \$50,000, \$100,000, \$500,000 or you may go broke.

Career path

Stockbrokers often go into sales management after five or more years of experience. Successful sales managers can progress to running a branch office or assuming senior level administrative responsibilities.

Where the Jobs Are

Analysts, M&A experts and traders tend to be uninterested in management careers. Analysts enjoy the analytical nature of their work, while traders and M&A experts enjoy the transactional nature of theirs. Thus, the career path is to become involved in bigger deals rather than progressing up a career ladder. There is no financial or career penalty if you decide not to pursue a management route.

Major employers: Who and where

Stockbrokers can work in virtually any city. Traders will find the majority of their opportunities are located in New York, Los Angeles or San Francisco. The greatest job opportunities for analysts and M&A experts are in New York.

Leading firms in the investment field include: Alex Brown & Sons, The Boston Company, Inc., Brown Brothers Harriman & Company, Chemical Bank, Dean Witter Reynolds, Dillon Reed, Donaldson Lufkin & Jenrette, Equitable Capital Management Corp., Goldman Sachs, Grubb & Ellis, Kidder Peabody, Lazard Freres & Company, Merrill Lynch, Neuberger & Berman, Nomura Securities International, John Nuveen & Company, Oppenheimer & Company, PaineWebber Inc., Piper Jaffray Inc., T. Rowe Price, Primerica Inc., Reliance Group Holdings, Salomon Brothers, Inc. and Smith Barney.

Resources

Some key employers

Alex Brown & Sons
135 East Baltimore Street
Baltimore, MD 21202
301-727-1700

Reliance Group Holdings
55 East 52nd Street
New York, NY 10055
212-909-1100

Salomon Brothers, Inc.
2 New York Plaza, 33rd Floor
New York, NY 10004
212-783-7000

The Boston Company, Inc.
1 Boston Place
Boston, MA 02108
617-722-7000

Brown Brothers Harriman & Company
59 Wall Street
New York, NY 10005
212-483-1818

J. P. Morgan
23 Wall Street
New York, NY 10015
212-483-2323

Associations

National Associations of Securities Dealers, Inc.
1735 K Street NW
Washington, DC 20006
202-728-8000

Securities Industry Association
120 Broadway
New York, NY 10271
212-608-1500

Financial Analysts Federation
5 Boars Head Lane
Charlottesville, VA 22901
804-977-6600

Security Traders Association
1 World Trade Center
Suite 4511
New York, NY 10048
212-524-0484

Publications

Barron's National Business &
Financial Weekly
420 Lexington Avenue
New York, NY 10170
212-808-7200

Financial Analyst's Journal
1633 Broadway, Suite 1602
New York, NY 10019
212-957-2860

Investment Dealer's Digest
2 World Trade Center
New York, NY 10048
212-227-1200

Futures
Futures Magazine, Inc.
250 South Wacker Drive
Suite 1150
Chicago, IL 60606
312-977-0999

Chapter 15

Franchise Opportunities

For the entrepreneur-minded who don't want to assume all of the risks, buying a franchise is a perfect compromise. You have all of the benefits of ownership, while participating in an estabished business that has proven to work in the past. During times of economic uncertainty, Americans show an inreasing interest in franchising.

People are attracted to franchising opportunities for a variety of reasons. Being laid off once or twice can make people gun-shy about working for a large corporation. Franchising offers you the chance to have greater control over your life. How well you do is determined by your own individual efforts. However, this does not mean that you will be working fewer hours. In fact, the opposite is often true.

People are also drawn to franchising because of a desire for more independence in their lives. Whether becoming a franchisee will satisfy this desire depends on the type of franchise you purchase. Some franchises, especially those that are relatively new and growing quickly, seek franchisees who are innovative and able to suggest and implement new ideas.

However, the majority of franchises expect you to conform to their way of doing business and are not very tolerant of individual innovation. Some discourage it, and others simply don't allow people to deviate from established procedures.

Most franchisees accept the fact that there are procedures they must follow, even if they don't understand them. This is one of the key differences between a franchisee and a true entrepreneur. The franchisee reduces his or her risk by following procedures that have been successful in the past. If your last corporate job left you with a complete distaste for following anyone's rules, you may find franchising to be frustrating. If this is the case, you may discover greater satisfaction and independence by starting your own business. However, it's good to remember that with the increase in independence comes a commensurate increase in risk.

What's hot and why

The primary method by which many American businesses are growing is franchising. By franchising, companies can expand faster than if they opened up company-owned shops one unit at a time. While many companies reported flat or declining sales, the sales of the nation's 542,000 franchise outlets rose 6.1 percent in 1991. Since growth is the lifeblood of industry, franchising should continue to be a hot opportunity in the 1990s.

Obviously there are hot and *not-so-hot* franchise opportunities. While a McDonalds franchise can be a license to print money, they are hard to come by and very expensive. One of the top franchises in the 1980s, Blockbuster Video, is continuing to expand and is dominating the video rental business. One good way to identify hot areas of franchising is to focus on trends. For example much has been written about how Americans are focusing on family values in the 1990s. This has resulted in more people eating meals at home. The problem is that people don't have time to shop for food. The franchise "Take Out Taxi," which provides home delivery from local area restaurants, capitalized on this trend.

Another hot franchise idea builds on the concept that a one-stop outlet, offering convenient hours and such services as fax machines, copies, postage stamps and mailboxes, would fill a niche. The franchise Mailboxes Etc. has been growing rapidly, primarily in urban areas. Finally, don't underestimate more traditional opportunities, such as the International House of Pancakes. IHOP operates a new outlet for six months before selling the franchise. This allows the restaurant to become established in the community during the very crucial early days. The company's support of its franchisees has increased average sales from $659,000 to $845,000. With plans to open 25 to 35 new outlets a year, the company has an obvious growth strategy.

Breaking in

How do you find and choose a franchise? Fortunately, since franchise success is dependent upon opening new units, it's easy to find out where the opportunities are. *The Wall Street Journal* runs a weekly section on franchising opportunities. Perusing the ads will give you a quick sense of the myriad of available opportunities. It really is surprising how much of American business is franchised. Deciding between hotels, copy centers, restaurants and employment agencies can be somewhat bewildering. Thus, you'll want to do a lot of research before committing yourself.

Although the risks of franchising are considerably less than starting a business from scratch, franchises sometimes go out of business. The most common reasons for franchise failure are an unproven business format, a bad choice of franchisees, poor quality control at the franchised outlets and a lack of adequate marketing support.

One of the best methods to learn about a particular franchise opportunity is to talk with someone currently in the business. It's most valuable to visit the business. Pick a time when business is slow and ask to speak with the owner. You'll be pleasantly surprised at the friendliness and receptivity most franchisees show when discussing their businesses.

Where the Jobs Are

While you shouldn't expect the franchise owner to pull out his or her financial balance sheet, you should be able to learn a lot of important information. Ask the owner why he or she chose this particular business. What type of support does the home office provide? Normally this will include marketing assistance. Find out how much you would have to contribute. What type of training would you receive, and is this training ongoing? Find out about protected territories. Your business will suffer if another franchise opens up a couple of blocks down the road. Are you buying a single business unit or the rights to open units within a geographic territory? How receptive is the home office to new ideas?

Once you've had this conversation, call the corporate office and ask to speak to the sales director. Ask this person a similar set of questions. If there is consistency between these two sets of answers, you can feel comfortable that you're getting a straight story.

Franchise costs and availability vary enormously. The average total investment for a franchise is $148,000, although the range is quite wide. For $12,000 you may be able to purchase a janitorial service that you can run from your home, while a McDonalds franchise is likely to set you back more than $500,000. In addition to the fee, a franchisee will typically pay a monthly royalty fee of 5 to 10 percent of gross sales and an advertising fee of 1 to 3 percent.

Having the funds to purchase the franchise is only the beginning. Considerable working capital is needed to get the venture under way. Franchising experts recommend that owners have six to nine months of overhead and salary in the bank in case unforeseen problems arise.

Although you may consider the costs to be high, remember that you may get what you pay for. The more established and successful the franchise is, the less risk there is to a new participant. Thus, the established franchises tend to charge more money, but they also provide the most comprehensive training and marketing assistance. Getting in on the ground floor of a successful franchise is your best bet, even though it carries the greatest risk. If you're considering buying a franchise, think about what type of business you would like to be in. After all you will be spending a lot of time there. If you don't like fast food, don't worry. There are plenty of other opportunities.

Compensation

Since you'll have to make a sizable investment, the first year won't be profitable. Make sure you've saved enough money to make it through. Franchises range enormously in their profitability. However, many franchises return to their owners profits in the $15,000 to $35,000 range per unit. This can often increase by 25 to 50 percent once the operational bugs are worked out. Big money is made by owning multiple units in a franchise. This is the long-term, 10-year strategy for success. Earnings well into the six figures are possible.

Career path

The good news is that you'll start at the top. The bad news is that you'll often have to do *all* of the jobs. In year one, be prepared to be both the boss and the dishwasher. Many franchises don't want absentee owners, and they stress the importance of learning the business from the ground up. Moreover, the first year is the riskiest so you'll want to minimize your overhead by doing most of the tasks by yourself. After the first year, you'll add to your staff and assume more management duties. If in 10 years you are successful in purchasing additional units, your role will become predominantly managerial. You'll focus on issues such as marketing and operations. Successful franchisees sometimes invest in other chains.

Major employers: Who and where

Franchise opportunities exist in every town and city in America. Check for leads in the business section of your local Sunday paper and the second section of *The Wall Street Journal.* The local chapter of the International Franchise Association may also be of help.

Resources

Associations

American Franchise Association
2730 Wilshire Boulevard, Suite 400
Santa Monica, CA 90403
213-829-0841

International Franchise Association
1350 New York Avenue NW, Suite 900
Washington, DC 20005
202-628-8000

National Association of Franchise Companies
221 Southwest 64th Terrace
Pembroke Pines, FL 33023
305-966-1530

Franchise Consultants International Association
5147 South Angela Road
Memphis, TN 38117
901-761-3085

Publications

Franchise
747 Third Avenue, 34th Floor
New York, NY 10017
212-319-2200

Franchising/Investments Around the World
P.O. Box 6996
Hollywood, FL 33081
305-966-1530

Franchising World
1350 New York Avenue NW, Suite 900
Washington, DC 20005
202-628-8000

Franchise Reporter
2730 Wilshire Boulevard Suite 400
Santa Monica, CA 90403
213-829-0841

Chapter 16

Health Care

We're getting older. The baby boom generation has moved from youth to middle age with the "golden years" not too far in the future. An unarguable fact of life is that as we grow older we are going to require more health care services. Yet while the health care industry is providing an increasing number of services, it is under pressure to reduce costs. The industry is going through exciting and challenging times and has a desperate need for capable people in some critical areas.

What's hot and why

Most everyone agrees that the health care industry is definitely one of the hot career fields for the future. The demand for services is almost guaranteed to increase, and yet a shortage of trained personnel persists. Among the hot jobs for the 1990s in health care are hospital administrators, nurses, and occupational and physical therapists.

Where the Jobs Are

Hospital administration. Managing a hospital is a demanding task that requires astute business judgment, excelent people skills and superior administrative capabilities. As hospitals are under pressure to control costs yet provide high levels of service, the hospital administrator is in an important position.

The hospital administrator reports to the board of directors of the hospital, and functions as a CEO or city manager would. The administrator's responsibilities include budgeting, hiring and training personnel, marketing, maintaining the physical facility and determining hospital procedure fees. In a large facility, an administrator may be responsible for a million-dollar budget and might supervise hundreds of employees.

The job has its frustrations. Doctors are primarily concerned with delivering the best possible patient care, and are less interested in management issues. Doctors and administrators often don't see eye-to-eye on a variety of issues. Thus, it takes a lot of tact and diplomacy to be an effective hospital administrator. However, despite these frustrations, the challenges of running a large health care facility can be rewarding, and the demand for experienced professionals will grow.

Nursing. Nurses play a critical role in the health care system, yet the field suffers from a chronic shortage. As the demand for nurses grows, many hospitals are raising their pay scales and trying to be more accommodating in the scheduling of hours.

Depending upon their training, nurses are either licensed practical nurses (LPNs) or registered nurses (RNs).

LPNs work for doctors or under an RN's supervision. They provide assistance in areas that require technical skills, but not the more extensive training of an RN. They take temperatures, administer medicine and assist in the transportation of patients.

Registered nurses perform specific medical tasks and manage LPNs, aides and hospital orderlies. Most RNs work in hospitals, although there are needs for LPNs and RNs in doctor's offices, community health programs and education.

Occupational therapy. This is one of the fastest-growing employment fields. Occupational therapists help patients who are mentally, physically or emotionally disabled. The therapist recommends activities that will help the patient regain physical capabilities, function independently or return to work.

The therapist uses a variety of activities to help the patient achieve these goals. They may include specific exercises designed to increase motor skills, strength, endurance, concentration or motivation. Some therapists concentrate on working with children while others work primarily with the elderly.

Therapists usually either work for a hospital, nursing home or rehabilitation center. This is a field that may be of particular interest for people interested in working part-time.

Physical therapy. Physical therapists work with victims of accidents and strokes, and the handicapped, assisting in the restoration of bodily functions and relieving pain. Therapists work closely with physicians in developing treatment programs that include exercises to increase strength, coordination and range of motion. Therapists use such tools as heat, massage and water to reduce pain or to improve physical capabilities.

Therapists often specialize in a particular group of problems such as sports injuries, geriatrics or cardio-pulmonary disease. The job is often physically demanding and can also be emotionally draining. The number of opportunities for physical therapists is expected to grow by 50 percent during the 1990s.

Breaking in

Hospital administration. Most hospital administrators have a business background that often includes an MBA degree or a CPA license. Some senior administrators gained their business experience in fields other than health care. Hospital administration is sometimes a consideration for individuals seeking to change industries.

Hospital administrators are recruited on college campuses by recruiting firms that specialize in the field, and by ads in local newspapers. A business degree is the preferred educational credential, although hospitals recruit individuals with various educational backgrounds if they have appropriate experience.

Where the Jobs Are

The interview focuses both on specific business skills and the candidate's philosophy toward health care in general. The business expertise hospitals look for includes finance, marketing and general management skills. Managing costs is an ongoing issue at virtually every hospital, so a strong background in finance or accounting is important. Hospitals are also finding that they have to aggressively market themselves in order to survive in the 1990s. Many hospitals offer an array of services unknown to the general public. For example, hospitals that have specialized treatment centers for children now rent billboard advertising space to increase awareness. Hospital administrators must have an appreciation for the role of marketing, and be creative in identifying methods in which the hospital's services can be marketed to the local community.

The hospital administrator must have exceptional interpersonal skills. The job requires the ability to work with a diverse group of people. Questions recruiters often ask in the interview include:

"What type of people *don't* you get along with?"

"Describe a situation when you had to get someone to do something they didn't want to do."

"How do you motivate people?"

"Describe your management style."

Nursing. In order to become an LPN, you must complete an approved practical nursing course and pass a written exam. It normally takes about a year to complete the program, and courses are offered through vocational schools, community colleges and hospitals.

RNs must graduate from an approved school of nursing and pass a licensing exam. Although a four-year degree is not required for licensing, it enhances your career options. A bachelor's degree is usually required for supervisory and administrative positions.

You will often be asked in the interview about your willingness to work rotating shifts. While you're better off being as flexible as possible, if you cannot work certain hours, you should discuss it up front so there are no surprises once you're hired.

Occupational/physical therapy. Occupational and physical therapists must have a certificate from an accredited educational program and must pass a licensing exam. The field is best suited to individuals who have a great deal of patience and a sincere interest in the welfare of others. Common interview questions include:

"What attracted you to this field?"

"What gives you the greatest source of satisfaction?"

"What job related activities do you find frustrating?"

Compensation

Hospital administration. Entry-level salaries range from $25,000 to $35,000. Most administrators with five to eight years of experience earn from $38,000 to $50,000. The head administrator at a large hospital can earn $150,000.

Nursing. LPNs can make from $18,000 up to the mid $30s. RNs start at approximately $21,000 and can make as much as $45,000. Both LPNs and RNs can increase their income significantly through overtime. RNs can increase their earnings if they become supervisors.

Occupational/physical therapy. Salaries range from $17,000 to $22,000. Experienced therapists earn from $28,000 to $32,000. Salaries normally top out in the mid- to high-$30,000 range.

Career path

Hospital administration. You typically begin your career in the marketing or finance department of a medium or large hospital. Over the next five to seven years, you will be rotated through a series of assignments, which will expose you to the variety of business functions in a hospital.

The next step is to be assigned as the number-two person in charge of a facility. Your duties may include overall responsibility during late evening shifts. In addition, you'll function as the general manager when the head administrator is absent. Success in this position can lead to the number-one position in a small to mid-sized hospital. It normally takes about 10 years to get to this level. A typical career path at this point is holding general management positions at increasingly larger facilities. The job often requires relocation. Flexibility is important if you want to be able to take advantage of every promotional opportunity.

Nursing. There are promotional opportunities for nurses interested in management. For example, an RN can be promoted to head nurse, then assistant director and ultimately, director of nursing services. By offering these promotional ladders, hospitals are often able to reduce the level of turnover, which has become a critical issue for many hospitals.

Occupational/physical therapy. Therapists generally remain therapists for the duration of their careers. Many work part-time and have little interest in traditional career progression. They enjoy the flexibility that the job allows. Therapists who do not have a four-year degree may be more limited in their career options. Some therapists do continue their education and eventually pursue careers in hospital administration.

Major employers: Who and where

Since hospitals are located in almost every city, many health care workers can choose where they live. Opportunities are particularly plentiful in smaller cities and towns in the Southeast and Midwest. Individuals pursuing hospital administration careers with large hospital chains may find that they must relocate frequently to both large and small cities. Nurses and therapists can usually choose where they wish to work.

In addition to hospitals, the following are often cited as offering particularly interesting careers: American Medical Holdings Inc., Amsco International-Healthcare Division, C.R. Bard-Home Health Division, Charter Medical Corp., Epic Healthcare Group, Glasrock Home Healthcare, HealthTrust Inc., Healthco International, Hospital Corporation of America, Humana, Manor Care Inc., Medco Containment Services,

National Health Laboratories, National Medical Care, National Medical Enterprises, NovaCare Inc., Rabco Health Services, U.S. Healthcare Inc., United Medical Corp., Universal Health Services.

For more information about various health care careers, contact the following associations: American College of Hospital Administrators, Chicago; National Health Council Health Career Program, New York; National League of Nursing, New York; National Association for Practical Nurse Education and Service, New York; American Occupational Therapy Association, Rockville, Md.; and the American Physical Therapy Association, Washington, D.C.

Resources

Some key employers

Amsco (infection control products)
500 Grant Street
Pittsburgh, PA 15219
412-338-6500

C.R. Bard, Inc. (medical and surgical equipment)
730 Central Avenue
Murray Hill, NJ 07974
908-277-8000

Charter Medical Corp.
(manages hospitals)
577 Mulberry Street
Macon, GA 31298
912-742-1161

Glasrock (rents health care equipment)
2233 Lake Park Drive
Smyrna, GA 30080
404-433-1800

Epic Healthcare Group
433 East Las Colinas Boulevard
Irving, TX 75039
214-869-0707

Montefiore Medical Center
111 East 210th Street
Bronx, NY 10467
212-920-4321

Catholic Medical Center of Brooklyn and Queens
88-25 153rd Street
Jamaica, NY 11432
718-657-6800

Mayo Foundation
200 Southwest First Street
Rochester, MN 55905
507-284-2511

Cedars-Sinai Medical Center
8700 Beverly Boulevard
Los Angeles, CA 90048
213-855-5000

Boston Hospital for Women
75 Francis Street
Boston, MA 02115
617-732-5500

Associations

American Physical Therapy Association
1111 North Fairfax Street
Alexandria, VA 22314
703-684-2782

American Occupational Therapy Association
1383 Piccard Drive, Suite 301
Rockville, MD 20850-4375
301-948-9626

American College of Healthcare Executives
840 North Lake Shore Drive,
Suite 1103W
Chicago, IL 60611
312-943-0544

National Federation of Licensed Practical Nurses
P.O. Box 18088
Raleigh, NC 27619
919-781-4791

National Association of Registered Nurses
1529 Huguenot Road, Suite 116
Midlothian, VA 22113
804-794-6513

National Association For Healthcare Recruitment
P.O. Box 5769
Akron, OH 44372
216-867-3088

Publications

American Journal of Occupational Therapy
1383 Piccard Drive, Box 1725
Rockville, MD 20850-0822
301-948-9626

Medical World News
Miller Freeman Publications
500 Howard Street
San Francisco, CA 94105
415-397-1881

American Journal of Nursing
555 West 57th Street
New York, NY 10019-2961
212-582-8820

Hospitals
American Hospital Publishing
Company
211 East Chicago Avenue
Chicago, IL 60611
312-440-6800

Chapter 17

Human Resources

Human resources, or personnel as it's traditionally referred to, is undoubtedly one of the corporate functions that has changed the most in the past 15 years. Once personnel was largely a dumping ground for individuals who hadn't experienced much success in their original careers, and employees were mostly accountable for tasks such as organizing the company picnic. Needless to say, they had only a nominal role in the management of business.

The genesis of HR as an important management function stems from the critical role it played during the peak years of labor management in the 1960s and 1970s. Dealing effectively with unions, and creating an environment that would discourage employees from unionizing all fell to specialists within the personnel function. These professionals were dealing with hard, pragmatic issues that affected the company's bottom line. This was quite different from the traditional personnel employee whose major responsibilities were to make sure everyone was happy and to process paper.

What's hot and why

There continues to exist a shortage of top-notch professionals in the field. People with strong technical skills and the ability to interface with senior line managers are in demand. The HR manager is the adviser to senior managers. In companies such as Apple Computer, few business decisions are made without HR's input. Elevating the credibility of the HR function to this point is what the new breed of personnel professionals are all about.

The majority of challenges that corporate America has faced over the past 5 to 10 years have involved how we manage people. For example, the "merger mania" of the 1980s resulted in more mismatches than "synergies." Why? Companies paid far too little attention to whether people from different organizations could actually work together once the merger was completed. Senior management finally acknowledged that differences in company culture could sink a potential marriage if the issues weren't identified and carefully dealt with. Throughout the boom times of the 1980s, human resources managers aggressively addressed these issues and established credibility for their function on other issues, such as compensation, benefits and management development.

During the late 1980s and into the 1990s, corporations, under pressure to increase or maintain profitability, experienced countless reorganizations and layoffs. Again, human resources managers were successful in establishing credibility with line managers and playing a leadership role on these sensitive issues. The role of human resources within corporations changed dramatically and a need emerged for top-flight individuals. At some of the top MBA schools, careers in human resources are rivaling in popularity the more traditional MBA career paths.

Currently, the hottest areas of specialization are compensation, benefits and management development. Compensation and benefits are the two most technical areas.

Compensation. A compensation analyst focuses on how pay can be more closely linked to performance, and the role of bonuses, commissions and stock options in a total compensation package. He or she also spends considerable time monitoring salary trends. The issues are often quite complex. For example, starting salaries for top MBA students have been increasing at an average annual rate of 6 to 8 percent, while merit raises for current employees have been running at 3 to 5 percent. This means that a newly hired MBA may be making as much, if not more, than an experienced worker. This problem of "internal compression" cannot be easily resolved. If the company arbitrarily raises the salaries of the experienced workers, it throws their pay out of whack with other departments.

Compensation issues can affect a company's ability to recruit top people and often becomes a political issue as well. Thus, the compensation expert must not only have technical knowledge, but also must have tact and diplomacy.

Benefits. This is another area that requires technical expertise. A company's benefit program encompasses a variety of issues including health care and retirement programs. Health care costs continue to escalate and companies are under great pressure to contain them. However, simply cutting services and raising premiums is not a long-term answer. While some companies have adopted this strategy, they usually find that while it brings short-term relief, it severely limits the company's ability to recruit and retain personnel.

Thus, benefits managers are looking at a variety of alternative health care solutions. These include managed care programs, where in exchange for a guaranteed flow of business, the doctors and hospitals agree to provide services for reduced fees. Negotiating these contracts has been a hot area for benefits managers.

The issue of retirement programs is equally complex. Programs are required to meet a variety of federal and state laws, which change periodically. In addition, there are significant tax implications that require highly specialized knowledge. Benefits managers deal with issues such as: When can employees have access to their money? At what percentage should the company match an employees contribution? Does the company have enough funds committed to the retirement program to meet federal guidelines?

Management development. While the recruiting area brings new employees on board, training workers falls to the management development area. Increasingly, companies are realizing that having the *right* people in the *right* jobs at the *right* time can give them an edge over the competition. Additionally, many companies have discovered that recruiting experienced people into the organization is more disruptive than productive. The emphasis in the 1990s is on hiring entry-level people and grooming them to assume larger assignments.

Management development specialists provide two important services. First they train employees in a variety of areas. Some of the training is skills-oriented, such as how to operate a word processor or prepare a budget. The rest is management-oriented. These programs teach such things as how to motivate, discipline and manage other employees. The management development area identifies the training needs of the company and develops informative and comprehensive programs.

The second area in which the management development department provides crucial services is identifying top performers within the company. Far too often companies do not develop a consistent standard by which employees will be evaluated. As a result, personal favoritism and politics play a large role in who gets ahead. Corporations are realizing that in order to be successful in the 1990s they can't leave promotions up to chance.

The first step is to implement an evaluation process that is consistent throughout the organization. Management development surveys line managers to identify the traits and characteristics necessary for career success. Based on this information, career paths are developed and the skills necessary for career advancement are clearly spelled out. The management development department then will coordinate the process by which high-potential managers are reviewed by senior-level executives.

Breaking in

Some corporations actively recruit human resources students on university campuses. This is particularly true for the graduate school level. While there are prestigious graduate programs in HR, human resources recruiters favor students enrolled in MBA programs. They feel that an MBA puts an HR professional on an even footing with the line managers he or she will work with. Additionally, the business degree provides a broad-based business perspective that aids job performance.

Individuals interested in a career in compensation often start with a consulting firm after earning a graduate degree in business. Opportunities sometimes emerge in corporate compensation departments, so it's a good idea to contact employers in your area. Larger employers tend to offer better opportunities since they have greater resources at their disposal.

Recruiters will evaluate you on your quantitative and interpersonal skills, both of which are important for success. Quantitative skills are usually determined through your grades in subjects such as advanced math and statistics.

Entry-level recruiting for the benefits area is most commonly done by consulting firms. Firms such as Hewitt Associates recruit individuals who have majored in such subjects as mathematics. Since the field is dominated by finance and tax issues, MBA and JD programs are also a good source of talent. Some benefit departments recruit individuals with strong backgrounds in tax, and they hire from the CPA firms.

Management development departments are often staffed by individuals with Ph.D.'s in industrial and organizational psychology. Consulting firms look for individuals with strong backgrounds in writing and group presentations.

Compensation

Annual entry-level salaries for compensation, benefits and management development range, depending on education, from $25,000 to $48,000. After five to eight years, managers working for a corporation will be earning $40,000 to $75,000. Consultants can do slightly better. Department heads can earn $125,000, including bonuses, if they choose to work for a large corporation. Consultants who specialize in these fields can earn more than $250,000.

Career path

Long-term career success in any human resources job is largely dependent upon the ability to establish credibility with line managers. Human resources may be the power behind the throne but it is seldom the route to the throne itself. Thus, the ability to influence the decision-making of line managers is critically important. If an HR manager can establish a relationship with a key line manager, he or she can reap enormous career rewards.

The key to establishing these relationships is initiative. What are the issues facing the line managers and what is the people component in the issue? One of the complaints line managers often have about HR is that while they may be good at identifying problems, they are poor at recommending solutions. Successful HR managers excel at both.

In compensation, benefits and management development, you will typically start as an analyst. You will work on portions of a supervisor's project. Three to five years into the career, you will become involved in larger portions of a project and may supervise others. After 10 to 15 years of experience, you will be running the department as a director or vice president.

Major employers: Who and where

The best opportunities are with the larger corporations and consulting firms. You want to make sure that you work for a company that is committed to HR and has the financial resources to support it. Companies that are expanding quickly often have interesting opportunities. There are also a number of corporations that have established a reputation for being particularly supportive of their human resources departments.

Consulting firms worth checking out include: Hay Associates, Hewitt Associates, William Mercer & Co., Towers, Perrin, Forster & Crosby, Harbridge House, Temple, Barker & Sloan, Wyatt Associates, and A.T. Kearney.

Corporations with excellent reputations in human resources include: Abbott Laboratories, American Cyanamid, Apple

Where the Jobs Are

Computer, American Express, Anheuser-Busch, Baxter Healthcare, Clairol, Coca-Cola, Clorox, The Walt Disney Company, Frito-Lay, General Electric, General Motors, Hallmark Cards, Hewlett-Packard, IBM, Johnson & Johnson, S.C. Johnson & Son, Kraft General Foods, Eli Lilly & Co., Marriott Corp., Merck & Co., 3M, NationsBank, NCR, Pepsi-Cola, Philip Morris, Procter & Gamble, Teradata, Unilever, Union Carbide and Warner Lambert.

Resources

Some key employers

William M. Mercer Companies, Inc.
(employment benefit consulting)
1166 Avenue of the Americas
New York, NY 10036
212-345-7000

Towers, Perrin, Forster & Crosby, Inc. (management consulting)
245 Park Avenue
New York, NY 10016
212-309-3400

Abbott Laboratories
(pharmaceutical company)
95-25 149th Street
Jamaica, NY 11435
718-291-0800

American Cyanamid
(chemical company)
1 Cyanamid Plaza
Wayne, NJ 07470
201-831-2000

American Express Credit Corp.
1 Rodney Square
Wilmington, DE 19801
302-594-3350

Associations

Society for Human Resource Management
606 North Washington Street
Alexandria, VA 22314
703-548-3440

Employment Management Association
4101 Lake Boone Trail
Raleigh, NC 27607
919-787-6010

International Association for Personnel Women
P.O. Box 969
Andover, MA 01810-0017
508-474-0750

Association of Human Resource Professionals
P.O. Box 801646
Dallas, TX 75380
214-661-3727

Publications

Employee Benefit News
Enterprise Communications, Inc.
1165 Northchase Parkway,
Suite 350
Marietta, GA 30067
404-988-9558

HR Magazine
Society for Human Resource
Management
606 North Washington Street
Alexandria, VA 22314
703-548-3440

HR News
Society for Human Resource
Management
606 North Washington Street
Alexandria, VA 22314
701-548-3440

Personnel
135 West 50th Street
New York, NY 10020
212-903-8389

Chapter 18

International

International assignments used to be a little suspect. Being out of sight and out of mind was a concern for many managers. This skepticism was not unwarranted; many companies paid scant attention to their international operations, and the international departments were sometimes staffed with individuals who were not successful in previous jobs.

Times have changed. Today, the greatest opportunities for many companies are coming from international markets. International jobs are now considered plum assignments. In some companies it is virtually impossible to ascend to the top positions without a tour of duty overseas.

The reason for this is that we are functioning in an international economy. The collapse of the former Soviet Union heralded a new era of economic opportunity for Eastern Europe. The Pacific Rim countries continue to provide some of the greatest opportunities and competitions to workers in the United States. Latin American countries are becoming more stabilized, and are eagerly courting Western businesses with promises of inexpensive labor.

Where the Jobs Are

Manufacturing has increasingly become international, with many different countries contributing parts used in the final product. This can cause confusion about whether a product is Japanese, American, Korean or French. This issue became clear during recent hearings on import tariffs on foreign cars. The hearings demonstrated that there is no longer such a thing as an American or Japanese car, since the parts are made in a variety of countries. Parts for American cars are often produced in Asia, and automobiles with Japanese names are manufactured in Kentucky.

What's hot and why

Companies such as Coca-Cola, Philip Morris and countless smaller firms are convinced that the future lies in overseas expansion. However, doing business in Beijing or Moscow is very different from doing business in St. Louis or Los Angeles. Mastering different cultures, languages and business practices will be critical for success.

International career opportunities are likely to remain hot throughout the 1990s and beyond as there continues to be a shortage of people with international business experience. The shortage exists because most American business people speak only English, and have worked solely in the United States. In order to be effective internationally, you must have spent enough time in a foreign country to learn its culture. Developing international business skills takes time, and those people who make the investment will be in demand.

The hottest areas for international opportunities are likely to be in Eastern Europe, Asia and Latin America. Language barriers and a lack of familiarity with the region will make qualified candidates scarce. Of the three areas, Latin America will probably be the easiest for individuals to break into because the cultural differences are not as great as they are in some areas of Eastern Europe and Asia, and Spanish is one of the easier languages to master.

Although there are many different international jobs, two areas offer the greatest amount of growth. As companies seek to expand, financing this growth will require the services of the international banker. Secondly, selling products overseas requires an understanding of foreign cultures, customer relations and import/export regulations. Individuals with backgrounds in international marketing will be in demand.

Breaking in

International bankers are either promoted from within a bank or hired directly into the international department. A bachelor's degree is required, and many international bankers also have an MBA degree. Banks often don't require employees to speak a foreign language before sending them overseas; instead, they enroll employees in intensive language classes prior to the assignment.

Recruiters look for individuals who demonstrate a sincere interest in international assignments, cultural flexibility and a willingness to travel extensively. The demands of the job often require time away from home for extended periods. While the image of international travel may be glamorous, it can be very demanding. Since international assignments are sometimes unpredictable, banks look for flexible, adaptable people.

Marketing opportunities are diverse. Companies often look for individuals who have lived overseas. Two years is generally the minimum, and fluency in the country's native language is usually required.

In the United States, there are a small number of MBA programs that have a specific international focus. The American Graduate School of International Management in Phoenix, The Lauder School in Philadelphia and the University of South Carolina in Columbia are three of the best.

Compensation

An individual recruited directly out of graduate school into the international department of a bank will earn $35,000 to

$50,000. Experienced international bankers earn $50,000 to $85,000. A senior vice president, who is in charge of all of the bank's activities, may earn a six-figure salary.

International marketers directly out of school will earn $22,000 to $35,000 with a smaller company, and $40,000 to $55,000 with a large marketing corporation. Individuals with 5 to 10 years of experience typically earn $50,000 to $85,000. Bonuses can add 20 to 30 percent to the base salary. The head of international marketing can earn $150,000.

Career path

Many bankers spend three to five years in an international assignment and then rotate into a different department in the bank. Other bankers spend their entire careers overseas, rotating through assignments in a number of countries.

Many marketing organizations view international experience as crucial for their future senior managers. International projects are often used as developmental assignments for managers being groomed for the top jobs. People move in and out of international assignments.

Major employers: Who and where

Companies with interesting international opportunities include the following: Alberto-Culver, American Cyanamid, Atlantic Richfield, Baxter International, Chrysler, Coca-Cola, Corning Inc., Dow Chemical, Exxon Corp., Ford Motor Company, General Electric, General Mills, General Motors, IBM, Merck & Co., NCR, Philip Morris, Texaco, and Warner Lambert.

Individuals interested in international banking assignments might wish to investigate the following: BankAmerica, Bankers Trust, Barclay's Bank, Chase Manhattan, Chemical Bank, Citicorp., Dai-Ichi Kangyo, Dominion Bankshares, Manufacturers Hanover, J.P. Morgan, Primerica Corp., Sanwa Bank, Wachovia and the World Bank.

Resources

Some key employers

Alberto-Culver (hair care products)
2525 Armitage Avenue
Melrose Park, IL 60160
708-450-3000

Atlantic Richfield Company
(petroleum products)
515 South Flower Street
Los Angeles, CA 90071
213-486-3511

American Cyanamid
1 Cyanamid Plaza
Wayne, NJ 07470
201-831-2000

Baxter International
(medical care products)
1 Baxter Parkway
Deerfield, IL 60015
708-948-2000

Barclay's Bank
75 Wall Street
New York, NY 10265
212-412-4000

The Dai-Ichi Kangyo Bank
770 Wilshire Boulevard
Los Angeles, CA 90017
213-612-6400

Associations

American Society of International Executives
18 Sentry Parkway, Suite 1
Blue Bell, PA 19422
215-540-2295

Federation of International Trade Associations
1851 Alexander Bell Drive
Reston, VA 22091
703-391-6106

United States Council for International Business
1212 Avenue of the Americas
New York, NY 10036
212-354-4480

Institute of International Bankers
280 Park Avenue, 4th Floor
New York, NY 10017
212-983-1066

Publications

Business International
Business International Corp.
1 Dag Hammarskjold Plaza
New York, NY 10017
212-750-6300

Overseas Business
Cara Communications Limited
100 Court Avenue, Suite 312
Des Moines, IA 50309
515-282-2888

International Business
American International
Publishing Corp.
500 Mamaroneck Avenue,
Harrison, NY 10528
914-381-7700

The International Executive
P.O. Box 408
Sarnac Lake, NY 12983
518-891-1500

Chapter 19

Law

For many years it appeared that lawyers were above the problems that plagued ordinary business people. Regardless of what happened in the economy, the popular thought was there would always be a need for lawyers. Today, the law has become a field of specialization. There is no longer such a thing as a "generic" lawyer. Lawyers specialize in small business, tax, litigation, family law and countless other areas.

The most important change that has affected the legal profession is the increasing awareness that the practice of law must be run as a business. Historically, many lawyers looked down their noses at individuals involved in the sullied world of "commerce." Today's lawyer realizes that simply practicing law is not enough to ensure survival. The most successful lawyers in the 1990s will be those who manage their activities as a business. Accounts receivable and accounts payable have now become equally important as a lawyer's win/loss record. As the regulations governing how lawyers can market their services become less rigid, lawyers are aggressively using marketing to enhance their business. The emphasis on the lawyer as a business person also accounts for the recent emergence of many joint MBA/JD graduate programs.

What's hot and why

Law will probably always be a hot career path because, like it or not, our society requires the services and expertise of lawyers. We are becoming an increasingly litigious society, and we rely on lawyers to help iron out the differences we have with each other.

While becoming a lawyer may not be a guaranteed passport to riches in the 1990s, despite a plethora of bad lawyer jokes, it is a profession that maintains a high level of prestige.

The law has become more specialized. In the 1980s, specialists in the area of mergers and acquisitions were in great demand. The excesses of the 1980s have given rise to some of the hot areas in the 1990s, such as bankruptcy, tax, and the "workout" segment of real estate. This latter specialization disposes of the office complexes and other real estate ventures that were misguidedly built in the late 1980s. In 1992, industry observers began to notice a small wave of consolidations in certain industries. This may indicate that mergers and acquisitions specialists will again be in demand in the mid-1990s. Divorce lawyers and criminal attorneys tend not to be affected by swings in the economy. These two fields are consistently the most stable in the legal profession.

Breaking in

Your career options will be initially determined by which law school you go to and how well you do. The top firms only recruit at the top schools and only interview students graduating near the top of their class. How successful you are in landing your initial job has less to do with your personality and interviewing skills than with the reputation of your school and your class rank. Thus, if you're serious about being a lawyer, you'll want to take advantage of every opportunity to improve your odds.

What law school you'll get into depends in large part on how well you do on the LSAT test. Signing up for one of the review classes is usually a good investment. The class will help you become familiar with the format of the test and increase your comfort level in answering the multiple-choice questions. The instructors will also provide you with helpful tips so that you don't waste valuable time during the test.

If the top schools are beyond your reach, focus on identifying schools that are located where you would like to live. Although these schools may not have as much national presence as the top-ranked schools, they are often highly effective in placing their graduates locally. Again, try for the best school in the region.

Law school is a lot of work and normally requires more effort than undergraduate school. It's usually not that the work is intellectually overwhelming, rather there's just so much of it. Hooking up with a strong study group can make the experience more rewarding and less arduous.

The summer internships after your first and second years at law school are very important. They allow you the opportunity to test out different firms, and hopefully will result in an offer of full-time employment.

Compensation

Your salary will be, in large part, determined by the type of firm you work for. At the top are the prestigious national firms, most often headquartered in New York. Starting salaries in the $80,000 range are common. The next tier are the top firms in smaller cities that may recruit on a regional basis. For example, a major St. Louis firm may pay $50,000 for a top graduate from a strong regional school. After these two levels the money declines greatly. Small firms, individual practitioners or specialty shops may only pay $30,000 or sometimes less.

Five to seven years into the profession, a lawyer with a regional firm may be earning $75,000 to $80,000. Their counterparts at prestigious national firms will often make $90,000 to $125,000. Top partners at national firms earn in the millions.

Career path

The career path in law has traditionally been highly structured. Graduate from law school, join a firm, work very hard for seven to eight years, and if you're lucky, be elected as partner and live happily ever after.

This unambiguous career path changed dramatically during the 1980s. Law firms began to focus on managing their firms as businesses, and individual lawyer productivity became a central issue. If you didn't pull your weight, you were quickly encouraged to seek opportunities elsewhere. Even partners weren't immune. The lifelong security associated with partnership became a relic of the past.

Still, the path to becoming a successful lawyer is relatively straightforward. Most future lawyers enter law school directly after completing their undergraduate degrees. There doesn't seem to be one particular degree that predicts success in law school, although a lot of law students have degrees in English and history. Since law students, and lawyers, write a great deal, this initial grounding in the liberal arts appears to be helpful.

The first few years of working as a lawyer are often a disappointment. There is very little arguing cases before juries and a lot of researching detailed aspects of the law. However, as uninteresting as this work is, it forces the young lawyer to gain an appreciation for detail, and gives him or her an understanding of how the law really works.

Law firms have two levels, partners and everyone else, and everyone—at least initially—wants to become a partner. The time it takes to become partner various considerably. Few, if any, firms promote people before six years, and a 12-year track to partnership would be considered lengthy. Some firms have the reputation for promoting most of their associates while others promote only a few. Law firm recruiters are often surprised that more prospective lawyers don't ask about this before joining the firm. Hints, subtle or otherwise, are provided along the way.

How can you increase your odds of becoming a partner? Bringing in new clients is the most obvious, although this is normally quite difficult for young lawyers. The key in the early years is to establish credibility with a great number of partners. Progression in a law firm is determined by the number of partners who want you to work on their cases. This poses an interesting challenge for successful lawyers. Since you can't work for everyone, how do you turn down a partner's request without alienating him or her? Tact and diplomacy are critical skills in order to successfully navigate these negotiations.

Working as an in-house counsel is an option some lawyers decide to pursue after their initial experience in a firm. Historically, in-house lawyers were perceived as individuals who did not make partner at their firms, and their credibility within the legal community was low. That has changed dramatically in recent years. Corporations rely on their internal lawyers to perform much of the legal work that was previously given to law firms. Additionally, corporate lawyers are now expected to aggressively manage the activities of the outside firms. The pendulum has begun to shift, with corporate attorneys now enjoying great credibility both within their corporations and among their legal peers.

Major employers: Who and where

The law is like most other professions, so you can pretty much practice wherever you choose. There are exceptions, since specialty practices such as entertainment or investments are clustered respectively in Los Angeles and New York.

Some of the top firms include the following:

Atlanta: Alston & Bird, Long & Aldridge, King & Spalding, and Powell/Goldstein.

Boston: Ropes & Gray, Hale & Dorr, Goodwin/Procter, Foley/Hoag, Mintz/Levin, Palmer & Dodge, Choate/Hall, Bingham/Dana.

Where the Jobs Are

Chicago: Seyfarth/Shaw, Keck/Mahin, Rudnick & Wolfe, Mayer/Brown, Schiff/Hardin, Jenner & Block, Hopkins & Sutter, Baker & McKenzie, Sonnenschein/Nath, Kirkland & Ellis, Wildman/Harrold, Sidley & Austin, McDermott/Will, Chapman & Cutler.

Los Angeles: Munger/Tolles, Latham & Watkins, Irell & Manella, Gibson/Dunn, Sheppard/Mullin, O'Melveny & Myers, Manatt/Phelps, Paul/Hastings.

New York: Donovan/Leisure, Shearman & Sterling, Kaye/Scholer, Winthrop/Stimson, Weil/Gotshal, Anderson/Kill, Stroock & Stroock, Davis/Polk, Proskauer/Rose, Kramer/Levin, Cleary/Gottlieb, Simpson/Thacher, Wachtell/Lipton, Rosenman & Colin, Kelley/Drye, Debevoise & Plimpton, Fried/Frank, Cahill/Gordon, Sullivan & Cromwell, White & Case, Skadden/Arps, Milbank/Tweed, Cadwalader/Wickersham, Cravath/Swaine, Dewey/Ballantine, Wilkie/Farr, Mudge/Rose, Lord/Day.

Washington, D.C.: Arent/Fox, Akin/Gumpt, Dow/Lohnes, Covington & Burling, McKenna & Cuneo, Shaw/Pittman, Arnold & Porter, Crowell & Moring, Wilmer/Cutler, Hogan & Hartson, Dickstein/Shapiro, Steptoe & Johnson.

Resources

Some key employers

Alston & Bird
3575 Koger Boulevard NW
Atlanta, GA 30309
404-881-7000

**Seyfarth, Shaw,
Fairweather & Geraldson**
55 East Monroe
Chicago, IL 60603
312-346-8000

**Skadden, Arps, Slate,
Meagher & Flom**
919 Third Avenue
New York, NY 10016
212-735-3000

**Donovan, Leisure, Newton
& Irvine**
30 Rockefeller Plaza
New York, NY 10019
212-307-4100

**Arent, Fox, Kintner,
Plotkin & Kahn**
1050 Connecticut Avenue NW
Washington, DC 20036
202-857-6000

Munger, Tolles & Olson
355 South Grand Avenue
Los Angeles, CA 90017
213-683-9100

Associations

American Bar Association
750 North Lake Shore Drive
Chicago, IL 60611
312-998-5000

National Lawyers Guild
55 Sixth Avenue
New York, NY 10013
212-966-5000

National Bar Association
1225 11th Street NW
Washington, DC 20001
202-842-3900

American Law Institute
4025 Chestnut Street
Philadelphia, PA 19104
215-243-1600

Publications

ABA Journal
American Bar Association
750 North Lake Shore Drive
Chicago, IL 60611
312-988-5000

Barrister
American Bar Association
750 North Lake Shore
Chicago, IL 60611
312-988-6114

Student Lawyer
American Bar Association
705 North Lake Shore Drive
Chicago, IL 60611
312-988-6114

American Lawyer
600 Third Avenue
New York, NY 10016
212-973-2800

Chapter 20

Outplacement

Interestingly, one of the fastest-growing jobs is in a field that did not even exist 20 years ago. While outplacement consultants perform an important role, they are often referred to as the corporate undertakers. As companies reduced their employment levels throughout the 1980s, outplacement consultants were used to assist displaced workers in finding new opportunities. Since companies will continue changing their work forces in the 1990s, outplacement consulting will also continue to be one of the hot career fields.

Outplacement came of age in the 1980s, in large part due to the unprecedented wave of mergers between major companies. In order to finance these acquisitions, corporations commonly took on large amounts of debt, which placed enormous pressures on the companies to reduce costs. This usually resulted in firing workers—one of the quickest ways a company can reduce its overhead.

However, since the wholesale firing of employees was not an image corporations wished to be associated with, a variety of terms became common. These included: downsizings, rightsizings, layoffs, restructurings and reductions in force. However, since these activities tended to affect older, more experienced workers, many companies felt vulnerable to charges of age discrimination and other lawsuits.

Hiring outplacement consultants reduced the likelihood of lawsuits since the displaced worker would be more likely to find employment quicker if he or she were offered assistance. Moreover, this move sent a positive message, to both the community and the remaining employees, that the company cared about the plight of those workers affected by a layoff.

Outplacement began as a cottage industry in the 1970s, primarily to serve the needs of senior-level executives who were involuntarily terminated. With the massive restructuring of the 1980s, the business evolved from an executive perk to a standard service, which was often expected when a company laid off people. It has even become common for hourly workers and support personnel to be offered a modified form of outplacement services.

Outplacement services vary considerably. Senior-level managers often receive individual counseling, personal offices, secretarial support and information on current openings. Mid-level managers are typically offered the opportunity to participate in a group outplacement workshop. These programs teach resume preparation and job-search techniques. Hourly workers will receive assistance with resume preparation and interview skills.

What's hot and why

The field is expected to grow throughout the 1990s. Outplacement services, which were once viewed as a perk for senior managers, have now become a standard part of the severance package. The business is still young and growing. Although two large firms, Drake Beam Morin and Right Associates, have emerged as industry giants, the outplacement field is still high-ly fragmented. Small firms often do quite well because of their local contacts. The two largest firms have spun off countless others, which now aggressively and successfully compete with their founders.

The hot jobs in outplacement are generally divided between marketing and counseling. Although counselors are encouraged to always be on the lookout for new business opportunities, their primary focus is on dealing with out-of-work clients. The marketing staff will normally not be responsible for working with individuals.

Counselors will work with 12 to 15 individuals at a time. Most of the work is performed one-on-one. It is difficult and challenging since clients are understandably upset about being terminated. Often the termination notice comes as a complete surprise, and the outplacement counselor must help the client deal with a range of emotions. The counseling often includes working with a client's family members.

The counselor helps the individual develop a job-search plan. This starts with a comprehensive review of the person's background. An individualized job-search plan is then implemented, with the outplacement firm providing administrative support along with personal counseling. Since the job search can be an inherently lonely and frustrating experience, the counselor plays a valuable role in helping the client maintain his or her motivation. The counselor also provides advice on salary negotiations, suggesting that the client doesn't jump at the first offer.

Obviously all of this support does not come without a price. A standard fee for outplacement services is 12 to 15 percent of the client's salary. Since clients often are older, experienced, and highly compensated, this can be quite expensive.

Selling these outplacement services is the role of the marketing staff. It's similar to selling other big-ticket items such as consulting services or computers. Outplacement firms market their services exclusively to corporations. They will not accept fees from individuals. Thus, the marketing staff must be adept at organizing meetings with the vice president of human resources, who is the key decision-maker in the purchasing of outplacement services.

The VP of human resources wants to know what the company will be getting for its money. Outplacement is usually sold on two premises. First, outplacement services will help laid-off employees find jobs more quickly. No companies want their former employees to be destitute and living on the street. Additionally, if the individual receives support on how to conduct a job search, he or she is less likely to sue the company for wrongful discharge. Secondly, offering outplacement sends a very positive message back to the employees who are still on the job.

A marketer spends the majority of his or her time calling on corporations. He or she may have to explain the concept of outplacement to a personnel chief who has never used the service before, or, on another call, compete against outplacement services offered by a competitor. As the field has matured, the competition has increased. This has led marketers to "unbundle" their services. Instead of offering one program, outplacement firms now offer an array of services tailored to meet a variety of budgets. Marketers are responsible for identifying trends, developing the overall marketing strategy and selling the programs to corporations.

Breaking in

Outplacement tends to be a second career for most people. Since the client is usually a person with 20 or more years of experience, recent graduates have difficulty establishing credibility.

Counselors have a variety of backgrounds. Many have a master's degree or Ph.D. in psychology, or have held human resources positions with other corporations. Often counselors have personally experienced layoffs, making them empathetic to the individuals they work with. All counselors share a deep compassion for people, and an interest in career management issues. They are effective listeners, allowing recently laid-off workers to vent their frustrations. The job can be enormously demanding. However, the satisfaction that comes from helping an individual find new employment is very gratifying. Counselors also need to have an in-depth understanding of careers in a variety of industries. They must be knowledgeable about job-search strategies and be able to help clients overcome hiring objections.

Many counselors start as part-time contract workers for an outplacement firm. It is difficult to predict workloads so outplacement firms keep their permanent staff as lean as possible. In times of peak demand, outplacement firms draw from a roster of part-time counselors. These contract workers are normally certified by the outplacement firm and complete one to two weeks of training.

Most outplacement marketers have experience in selling a product to a corporation. Graduates of companies known for their sales expertise, such as Xerox and IBM, are found in the outplacement field, as are former members of the executive recruiting industry. As the economy softened in the late 1980s, causing companies to rely less on headhunters, many former recruiters switched over to the outplacement field.

As outplacement grows, it will become an attractive opportunity for former corporate human resources managers and university placement directors. Contract workers are often elevated to full-time status when business expands. Firms are listed in the yellow pages or in the *Directory of Outplacement Consulting Firms* published by Kennedy & Kennedy, Fitzwilliam, N.H.

Compensation

Counselors start in the $40,000 to $50,000 range. The sales staff is paid $35,000 to $45,000 plus bonuses, based on productivity. Contract workers are paid a daily fee ranging from $300 to $500. Counselors with five years of experience can earn $55,000 to $65,000. Few counselors earn more than $75,000. An experienced salesperson can earn $65,000 to $75,000. Sales job salaries top out around $80,000. Six-figure incomes are usually restricted to owners and managers of multiple offices.

Career path

Many people begin their careers as part-time contract employees. Counselors and marketers usually start as associates and can be promoted to vice president in one to two years. The VP title is largely ceremonial. Its chief benefit is in establishing credibility with individual clients and corporate HR heads. The title of senior vice president indicates responsibility for a particular function, such as marketing, program development or administration. The general manager of the firm normally carries an executive VP title, and is almost always from the marketing side of the business. A few large firms have regional managers who are responsible for the activities of 3 to 12 offices.

Since the business is still growing quickly, a large number of outplacement employees have quit their firms to go out on their own. This has become a significant issue for the largest firms, which find that they are losing some of their best talent. Starting your own firm may be the choice you ultimately make.

Major employers: Who and where

As the popularity of outplacement has spread, firms have sprouted up in most major cities. Concentrations of firms exist in New York, Los Angeles and Chicago. The two largest firms are Drake Beam Morin, and Right Associates. Other leading firms include: Lee Hecht Harrison; Challenger, Gray & Christmas; Murray Axmith & Associates; King, Chapman, Broussard & Gallagher; Jannotta Bray & Associates; and Manchester Mainstream Access.

Resources

Some key employers

Drake Beam Morin, Inc.
100 Park Avenue
New York, NY 10017
212-692-7700

Jannotta Bray & Associates
20 North Wacker Drive, #3600
Chicago, IL 60606
312-443-1401

Lee Hecht Harrison, Inc.
200 Park Avenue
New York, NY 10166
212-557-0009

Right Associates
1234 Market Street
Philadelphia, PA 19107
215-988-1588

Associations

Association of Outplacement Consulting Firms
364 Parsippany Road
Parsippany, NJ 07054
201-867-6667

National Association of Career Development Consultants
1707 L Street NW, Suite 333
Washington, DC 20036
202-452-9102

Publication

Directory of Outplacement Consulting Firms
Kennedy Publications
Templeton Road
Fitzwilliam, NH 03447
603-585-6544

Chapter 21

Pharmaceutical Companies

Few industries can match the explosive growth of pharmaeutical companies. The pharmaceutical industry is full of enormous risk and potential. The investment in new drugs is huge, but so are the potential profits. Successful drugs are protected under patents that can yield enormous profits until they expire. The pharmaceutical industry is continually on the outlook for the next blockbuster drug, and no other industry plows as much of its profits back into research and development. The industry is made up of small entrepreneurial companies and huge multi-billion dollar corporations.

Many companies compete to invent the next miracle drug. Smaller companies are more informal and put a greater emphasis on the ability to perform a variety of tasks. For example, a salesperson may also be involved in the customer service area or might pitch in when there is a backlog in the distribution department. Larger organizations, traditionally tend to develop specialists, although this is changing some-what.

What both large and small pharmaceutical companies share is an emphasis on research and development. Science is the key to success for the drug companies. Great efforts are made to recruit, train and retain the top biologists, chemists and other science graduates from the nation's top schools. Traditionally, pharmaceutical companies have been founded by scientists, who still dominate senior-level positions throughout the industry.

After R&D, the pharmaceutical firms are driven mostly by marketing. The companies spend millions of dollars in advertising and promotions geared toward the medical profession. The sales forces of the pharmaceutical companies are some of the best-trained and best-equipped in any industry.

What's hot and why

The pharmaceutical industry is hot for four primary reasons. First, there is an explosion of new drugs on the market. Illnesses we "just had to live with" in the past can now be alleviated through drug therapy. Secondly, as the population continues to age, the demand for drugs has increased. Then, because the pharmaceutical industry is enormously profitable, a lot of money is used on R&D, marketing and human resources projects. It is much more enjoyable to work for a company that has the cash to invest in its people and programs.

Finally, the pharmaceutical companies are some of the best-managed companies in the nation. Companies such as Merck, which has won *Fortune* magazine's best-managed company award for the past five years, are leaders in innovative management techniques. Its reputation for training and developing people is excellent. This makes the pharmaceutical companies an exceptional place in which to start your career. Let's take a look at some of the hot opportunities.

Research and development. Pharmaceutical companies need individuals with strong biology and chemistry backgrounds. The environment of the R&D department is often similar to that of a university. While there is a great amount of pressure to discover the next hot drug, the departments themselves are characterized by informality and collegiality. Since many scientists working in R&D departments would have otherwise worked in academia, pharmaceutical companies often try to make their R&D centers resemble academic environments. R&D jobs are best suited for individuals who have an interest in working on practical applications to scientific problems.

Sales. This is an equally hot area in the pharmaceutical field, and one in which companies put a lot of effort and money. Doctors rely on the pharmaceutical reps to keep them up to date on new drugs and changes in technology. It is surprising how much influence the sales reps have on what drugs the doctor prescribes. However, selling to doctors is not easy. Physicians have only a limited amount of time between patient visits, so the rep must be adept at establishing credibility and making the sales pitch quickly. Physicians are also demanding customers. They ask in-depth questions, which requires the rep to be thoroughly knowledgeable.

Training. Few businesses emphasize training as much as pharmaceutical companies do. Continuing education is an important competitive advantage. Trainers must teach sales reps how to become a combination of scientist, business strategist and persuasive communicator. Increasingly, companies such as Syntex Labs are using home computers to train their sales forces on changes and advances in drug therapy. Since calling on doctors can often be intimidating and requires a sophisticated level of product knowledge, Park-Davis's junior sales reps practice presentations before residents from two major hospitals. The exercise instills confidence and increases sales reps' product knowledge.

Human resources management. In addition to R&D and sales, the industry offers exciting opportunities for individuals interested in human resources management. Companies such as SmithKline Beecham have developed reputations for expertise in helping organizations manage change. This company, which experienced a restructuring, plant closing and merger all in one year, realized that its human resources department was critical in order to manage the "people issues." As a result, SmithKline added additional personnel to an already strong HR department and created the highly regarded "Managing Change" training program. This innovative program helped employees deal with the emotional issues associated with restructuring. The program became an integral part of Smith-Kline, and underscored the important role that human resources played in the organization.

SmithKline is not unique is this respect. Merck & Co. realized that one challenge it faced was retaining its growing female work force. The human resources staff developed an innovative childcare policy and designed trendsetting programs in the areas of job sharing, flextime and flexible benefits. Companies such as Merck and SmithKline look for individuals who have a solid foundation in the fundamentals of human resources, but who also are willing to challenge the status quo.

Plant management. With an emphasis on quality, the pharmaceutical industry is also exciting for those interested in plant management. Managers at Johnson & Johnson's Sherman, Texas, medical plant were among the first to use teams of workers to improve quality. Their efforts were recognized in 1991 when *Industry Week* cited the plant as one of the best-managed in the nation. The plant management career requires an engineering degree and frequent relocations to smaller cities. However, a plant manager's job is a true general management position, which some might find highly appealing.

The pharmaceutical industry is also attractive to people who want to work in more than one specialty. Companies such as Warner Lambert are committed to developing multidimenional managers through job rotations. All managers receive training in leadership, negotiations and interpersonal effectiveness. Job assignments draw candidates from a wide diversity of backgrounds. For example, researchers are encouraged to assume non-research positions and teach university-level courses. For individuals who are not afraid of challenging themselves in areas outside of their expertise, pharmaceutical companies may be the most innovative employers in the 1990s.

Breaking in

For R&D jobs, pharmaceutical companies recruit extensively on college campuses, especially at the graduate level.

Where the Jobs Are

Graduate students in chemistry, biology and other scientific fields consider pharmaceutical firms some of the most desirable recruiters on campus. Students who may have envisioned themselves working in academia find the intellectual challenge and paychecks of the pharmaceutical firms very enticing.

Recruiters tend to scout at schools that have reputations for excellence in a particular field of study. Company representatives call professors for recommendations. Thus, if you are about to graduate, make sure that the professors in your area know about you and your career goals.

The interviews are anticlimatic for many candidates. Since the emphasis is on technical skills, the human resources department plays only a nominal role in the recruiting of R&D candidates. You're likely to spend most of your time with a lab supervisor or R&D director. In these conversations, the emphasis will be on how applicable your studies are to their research interests. Interviewing skills and business dress are less important than your product knowledge. To put it simply, you either have the necessary knowledge or you don't. Thus, the interview is usually a verification of your professors' recommendations.

The bulk of entry-level R&D jobs are filled by recruited college and graduate school students. Recruiters commonly look for individuals who have had some prior connection with the health care industry. This might include an undergraduate degree in the sciences, prior work experience in the health care profession or even having grown up in a medical family.

Jobs are advertised in trade publications and *The Wall Street Journal,* and are often listed with executive recruiters who specialize in the pharmaceutical industry.

In contrast to R&D jobs, great emphasis is placed on interviewing skills for sales jobs. Some pharmaceutical companies have candidates participate in mock sales situations to test skills. The interviewers are sometimes brusque in nature. This is done purposely, since selling to physicians is difficult and doctors are prone to dismissing sales reps who don't make their points quickly.

The pharmaceutical companies also place a great deal of weight on grades. They like to see people who have done well in a demanding science or technical discipline. Although the drug companies will hire liberal arts graduates, these students have to work harder to convince recruiters of their intellectual capabilities.

The emphasis on grades is directly related to the training demands of the pharmaceutical companies. The training is comprehensive and rigorous. Training emphasizes human anatomy, biology and the body's reaction to various chemical compounds. Thus, a grounding in the sciences is an advantage.

Other pharmaceutical companies hire experienced salespeople from other industries for their entry-level jobs. The industry has its fair share of people who received their original training at companies such as Xerox and IBM. While much of the sales recruiting is done at universities, there are continual openings as reps are transferred and promoted. An effective way to break in is to contact the local area sales manager. Very often these individuals are willing to meet you for an exploratory discussion, regardless of whether they have an opening.

Since human resources and plant positions generally require experience, most pharmaceutical companies do not recruit new college graduates for these jobs. However, the experience does not necessarily need to be in the pharmaceutical industry. Although ads are used to fill these positions, they are commonly listed with a recruiting firm that specializes in HR or plant management.

Compensation

Entry-level salaries for R&D range from $22,000 to $28,000 for people with bachelor's degrees and up to $55,000 for those with Ph.D.'s. You're likely to earn more money if you pursue a management career track rather than remaining in the lab. Many lab jobs top out at $55,000 to $65,000, while managers can command $75,000 to $100,000 in senior-level assignments.

Sales jobs start with an annual base salary of $22,000 to $26,000, plus a bonus and a car. Students with a graduate degree can sometimes command up to $32,000 in base salary. Experienced reps in the field will earn $35,000 to $75,000. It is rare for a field sales rep to earn more than $100,000.

Where the Jobs Are

Since pharmaceutical companies do not generally hire entry-level human resources or plant manager employees, salaries reflect individuals with five or more years of experience. Human resources jobs will range from $40,000 to $60,000. Plant supervisory jobs range from $35,000 to $70,000. The top HR job will pay $100,000 to $150,000, plus bonuses, at a large firm. Plant managers responsible for the overall activities of a manufacturing facility earn $75,000 to $95,000. Bonuses based on productivity can add up to 40 percent to the base salary.

Career path

R&D professionals often make the decision to spend their entire careers as research scientists. Progressive pharmaceutical companies have responded by not penalizing individuals who decide to remain in the lab. However, since most of these programs are new, individuals who opt for the management track generally still earn more money.

Career progression in R&D management is from lab tech (years one through three) to lab supervisor (years five through eight) to department head (8 to 10) to division R&D director (10-plus) to overall head of R&D. This last position is usually a vice president position and is generally obtained after 15 to 20 years of experience.

The sales career path is less linear since many companies make a specific effort to rotate sales personnel through a variety of staff assignments. A typical career path might include spending the first three years in one location. The promotion to sales supervisor might require a relocation. After another three years, you might be rotated into human resources. It's common for sales personnel to spend a year or two coordinating their company's college recruiting effort. After this assignment, you might be promoted back into the field as an area sales manager, and after another three years, you may be promoted to a regional sales manager. The top sales job usually is not obtained until 20 to 25 years into the career. Throughout your career you might be periodically posted to staff assignments designed to broaden your background. These may also include opportunities overseas. This is particularly popular with pharmaceutical firms that emphasize the development of global managers.

For example, Schering-Plough rotates managers through two- to five-year assignments in offices around the world. While the opportunities are challenging, they put enormous strains on both the manager and family. In addition to the normal challenges of learning a new assignment, they also must learn a new culture. However, given the increasingly international focus of the pharmaceutical industry, managers who are willing to invest a portion of their careers in international assignments are likely to reap substantial benefits down the road.

Major employers: Who and where

Many of the pharmaceutical firms have their headquarters in the Northeastern and upper Midwestern states but they're located in other areas of the country as well. Those who are interested in research and development positions may have to work out of corporate headquarters. But candidates who are interested in sales, human resources or plant management assignments may find opportunities in a variety of cities. Wherever you start out—whether in the field or the home office—be prepared to remain flexible as relocations are common in this industry.

Leading pharmaceutical companies you might want to check out include: Abbott Laboratories, Alberto-Culver, Alcon Laboratories, Inc., Allergan Inc., American Cynamid, American Home Products Corp., Amgen, Bausch & Lomb, Baxter Healthcare Group, Berlex Laboratories, Inc., Block Drug Co., Bristol-Meyers Squibb Co., Burroughs Wellcome Co., Carter-Wallace Inc., Chesebrough-Ponds, and Ciba-Geigy Corp.

You might also want to investigate employment opportunities at the following companies: Hoechst-Roussell Pharmaceuticals, Hoechst Celanése Corp., Merck & Co., Hoffman-

Where the Jobs Are

LaRouche, Johnson & Johnson, Lever Brothers, Eli Lilly Co., Marion Merrell Dow, McNeil Pharmaceutical, Miles Inc., Monsanto Inc., Pfizer Inc., Rexall Group, Rhone-Poulenc Inc., A.H. Robbins, Sandoz Inc., Schering-Plough Corp., SmithKline Beecham, Solvay America, Sterling Winthrop, The Upjohn Co., Warner Lambert Co., Whitby Pharmaceuticals, Whitehall Laboratories and Wyeth-Ayerst Laboratories.

Resources

Some key employers

Ciba-Geigy Corp.
444 Saw Mill River Road
Ardsley, NY 10502
914-478-3131

Allergan, Inc.
2525 DuPont Drive
Irvine, CA 92715
714-752-4500

American Home Products Corp.
685 Third Avenue
New York, NY 10017
212-878-5000

Bausch & Lomb
1 Lincoln First Sq., Box 54
Rochester, NY 14601
716-338-6000

Berlex Laboratories, Inc.
300 Fairfield Road
Wayne, NJ 07470
201-292-8048

Schering-Plough Corp.
One Giralda Farms
Madison, NJ 07940
201-822-7000

Associations

American Pharmaceutical Association
2215 Constitution Avenue NW
Washington, DC 20037
202-628-4410

Pharmaceutical Manufacturers Association
1100 15th Street NW
Washington, DC 20037
202-628-4410

Where the Jobs Are

Paternal Drug Association
1617 JFK Boulèvard
Philadelphia, PA 19103
215-564-6466

National Pharmaceutical Association
Howard University
Washington, DC 20059
202-328-9229

Publications

Pharmaceutical Processing
301 Gilbraltar Drive
Morris Plains, NJ 07950
201-292-5100

Journal of Pharmaceutical Sciences
2215 Constitution Avenue NW
Washington, DC 20037
202-628-4410

State Pharmaceutical Editorial Association Group
223 West Jackson Boulevard,
Chicago, IL 60606
312-939-7663

Pharmaceutical Technology
859 Williamette Street
Eugene, OR 97401
503-343-1200

Chapter 22

Public Relations

The Tylenol poisoning incident in the 1980s is an example of how important effective public relations can be to a company. Immediately upon the discovery that some bottles of the pain-reliever contained poisoned tablets, the parent company, Johnson & Johnson, quickly implemented an aggressive PR program. It positioned the firm as a concerned corporate citizen, intent on doing the right thing. This immediate action enabled the company to gain the support of the media and ultimately the public. Tylenol was removed from the shelves, remanufactured in tablet form and reissued in tamper-resistant bottles. Quickly the brand regained the market share it had enjoyed prior to the incident.

However, Johnson & Johnson's response to the Tylenol poisoning incident didn't just *happen*. The successful handling of the situation was due in large part to the credibility the PR department had established with the chairman. Thus, when the incident happened, the chairman listened to their advice on how best to proceed. It is in situations such as these that the public relations department shows how it can contribute directly to the bottom line.

Other companies have observed the way in which Johnson & Johnson handled the Tylenol incident and have increased their efforts. MCI, the long-distance carrier, believes that PR is integral to its business since key decisions that affect the company are made in a highly public forum. The more a company must rely on the public's approval to build business or increase prices, the more important the PR department is.

In another example, Dow Chemical, despite issues of public perception, has doubled its sales since 1987. Individuals considering careers in PR should examine companies prone to perception issues. These may be some of the most exciting places to work.

The health care industry has also realized the importance of PR. Health care suffers from an image problem that affects it in two important ways. Reimbursement from Medicare and Medicaid are heavily influenced by the government, which is now considering various forms of a national health care program. These issues have mobilized the health care industry to beef up its PR departments to make sure its point of view is clearly articulated. Secondly, a major source of financing for the hospitals is through individual or corporate donations. The image problems affect the receptivity of donors contributing money.

What's hot and why

Top among careers that don't seem to be popular with college students these days is public relations. It's clear that there is a demand for PR professionals, yet there continues to exist a shortage of talent. Granted, there are a lot of people who can write a press release or execute a PR strategy. However, people who can work with senior management on developing a PR strategy that can be integrated into the company mission are few. PR professionals are more than just good writers and the mission of PR is more than just to get the name of the company in the local, national and trade press.

As issues such as the environment, health and safety continue to be at the top of the public's agenda, CEOs will know that gaining and maintaining the public's trust is one of their key responsibilities. Advising corporate leadership on how best to handle these challenges will be a major opportunity for the PR professional. The question both CEOs and PR personnel ask is the following: "Is the profession attracting and developing the right group of people to handle the increased demands?" Thus far the answer is unclear. The trade publication *Public Relations Quarterly* cited that the greatest challenge to the profession is the shortage of talent. Thus, the potential for a career in PR is at an all-time high.

Careers in PR exist both in corporate PR departments and with public relations firms. Individuals tend to develop a specialization in a particular industry and may move back and forth between working for a company or a firm. Two top areas for PR are *investor relations* and *client interest representation* in Washington, D.C. PR managers working in Washington often serve as advisers to lobbyists. PR practitioners spend a great deal of time working with lawyers to anticipate what the company might be accused of. They construct "worst case" scenarios and develop strategies on how the client can best communicate his or her position through the media. The successful PR professional realizes that the public does not presume a company is innocent until it is proven guilty. The public is heavily influenced by what it reads and hears.

An effective PR strategy is built on speed and communication and requires developing an extensive network of contacts that can be mobilized quickly. This is especially true in Washington where "who you know" is critically important. Public relations has become a particularly attractive option for women, who now make up more than 55 percent of the PR population.

More so than many other functions, PR is wrestling with a variety of issues associated with change. The long-term success of PR will depend upon how it resolves the fundamental conflict between its traditional role as an apologist for management and its desired role as a strategic adviser. In order for PR to accomplish this task, it will need to attract individuals who can establish credibility with line managers and who are willing to be held accountable for measurable and meaningful results.

Breaking in

The recent trend toward recruiting of business school graduates is one visible sign that the industry is becoming more professional. PR practitioners must have a knowledge of psychology, sociology, economics and public opinion research in order to craft the message and communicate it in a way that the public will believe. Both firms and corporations are looking to their PR departments to back up their advice with specific expertise. Increasing pressure is on the PR community to show how effective PR has been in achieving tangible results.

Although the PR profession is attracting more business school graduates, the majority of people in the field are drawn from various communications jobs. At schools, public relations is usually taught as a part of a journalism or communications degree. This is a point of contention within the PR community. They feel that one of the most effective methods of upgrading professionalism is increasing the integrity of PR as an academic discipline. Thus far the academic community has not embraced such a concept.

About half of all PR professionals are former journalists who switched to PR because of increased compensation, job satisfaction and career advancement. College internships are a good way to break into the business. These are usually offered for credit rather than cash, and they give you a sense of what goes on in a PR department. They also can lead to full- time employment upon graduation.

Your interviewing skills will play an important role in getting hired. Recruiters often focus on how much you know about the field, since it is often misunderstood. Interviewers will ask you how well you function under pressure and about your knowledge of various industries in which they have clients. It's a good idea to research the firm prior to the interview.

Compensation

Entry-level salaries range from $18,000 to $24,000. Investor relations is the highest-paying PR specialty with a median income of $52,000, compared to $39,000 for PR in general. The demand for this type of PR professional is likely to grow with the further globalization of the financial markets. And, because investor relations requires that you speak the language of business, it is increasingly attracting business school and MBA students. Smaller financial firms, which must adopt a more comprehensive communications strategy in order to get their fair share of attention from the investment community, are also realizing the benefits of PR.

In recent years, PR executives who earned more than $100,000 per year either specialized in investor relations or were at the senior management level at a PR firm. Although attitudes are changing within corporations, PR is still underrated and does not pay as well as jobs in finance and marketing.

Career path

You may begin your career in PR writing press releases for a variety of clients. Within the first five years, you'll begin to develop an expertise in a particular industry. As your knowledge grows, you will be invited into client strategy sessions. Individuals with seven to nine years of experience are often either managing a mid-sized client or a significant portion of a major client. At this stage you may be supervising three to five employees.

Becoming a director in a PR firm normally takes about 10 years. Directors are responsible for the overall management of a large client. Directors report to vice presidents, if the firm is public, or partners, if it is private. The director level is normally achieved 15 to 20 years into the career.

Public relations is unique since people often leave the field for a number of years and then return. Many are writers, who often take leaves of absence to write books or return to journalism. Since PR attracts an eclectic group of people, this movement in and out of the profession is tolerated.

Major employers: Who and where

While smaller public relations agencies operate in many mid-sized cities, the majority of firms are in Los Angeles or New York. Chicago also has a number of highly regarded firms. Some of the top firms include: Addis & Reed, Ailes Communications, Inc., Aragon Consulting Group, Chester Burger & Company, Churchill Group/IPR, J.H. Clausen, Communication Associates, DeMarco & Associates, Dovetail Consulting, ICF Inc., Lammers & Gershon Associates, Hill & Knowlton, Inc., Ketchum Public Relations, Marketing Advisory Services, Thomas Poole & Associates, Rogers & Cohen, Ruder Finn, Strategic Management Resources, Bert Wallace & Associates and Somers White Company.

Resources

Some key employers

Ailes Communications, Inc.
440 Park Avenue South
New York, NY 10016
212-685-8400

Churchill Group/IPR
9575 Katy, Suite 390
Houston, TX 77024
713-781-0020

Hill & Knowlton, Inc.
420 Lexington Avenue
New York, NY 10017
212-697-5600

Ruder Finn
110 East 59th Street
New York, NY 10022
212-593-6400

Ketchum Public Relations
1133 Avenue of the Americas
New York, NY 10036
212-536-8800

Berkman & Daniels
1717 Kettner Boulevard
San Diego, CA 92101
619-234-6151

Associations

**International Public
Relations Association**
11350 McCormick Road
Hunt Valley, MD 21301
301-771-7305

**Public Relations Society
of America**
33 Irving Place
New York, NY 10001
212-995-2230

**Institute for Public Relations
Research & Education**
310 Madison Avenue, New
York, NY 10017
212-370-9353

**Public Relations Student
Society of America**
33 Irving Place
New York, NY 10001
212-995-2230

Publications

Public Relations Journal
33 Irving Place
New York, NY 10003
212-995-2230

PR News
127 East 80th Street
New York, NY 10021
212-879-7090

Public Relations Quarterly
44 West Market Street
Rhinebeck, NY 12572
914-876-2081

PR Reporter
P.O. Box 600
Exeter, NH 03833
603-778-0514

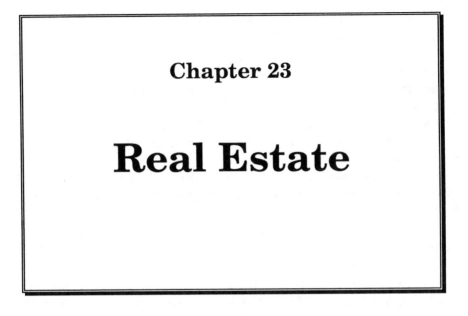

Chapter 23

Real Estate

Mention real estate and visions of Donald Trump often come to mind. While real estate investing has historically been one of the most popular avenues to wealth, the industry is often misunderstood. Although real estate is prone to economic booms and busts, it provides a variety of rewarding and challenging careers. Additionally, real estate offers some of the best opportunities for women looking to reenter the work force.

What's hot and why

In the late 1980s real estate opportunities vanished as many cities dealt with an oversupply of housing and office buildings. In the past five years, much of that oversupply has been taken care of and opportunities are again appearing.

The best real estate opportunities are in both commercial and residential real estate. Commercial development refers to business projects such as office buildings, office parks or shopping malls. Residential projects include single-family homes, condominiums and apartment units.

Residential real estate agents specialize in a particular community. To be successful, an agent must know about schools, taxes, traffic and other issues affecting property value, in addition to understanding economics. Established agents receive most of their business through referrals.

The best residential real estate jobs are in established upper-class neighborhoods or in newer developments. Check out neighborhoods near corporations. Since companies are frequently relocating employees, these neighborhoods can be quite active.

While residential real estate agents focus on a particular community, commercial real estate agents are national or international in scope. Commercial projects are large, complex and often take years to develop. A commercial agent will usually start with little more than a concept, which must be turned into a physical facility filled with tenants. While the profit potential is huge, millions of dollars are usually at risk. When you read about the enormous amount of money made and lost in real estate, the articles are typically referring to commercial real estate.

Aggressiveness, drive, salesmanship and tenacity are desirable traits for real estate agents, whether commercial or residential. However, given the complexity and enormous sums of money involved, the commercial real estate agent must have additional skills. These include a knowledge of finance, marketing and computer technology, and an overall broad-based appreciation of how real estate costs affect the company's profitability. As clients become more sophisticated, so must the commercial real estate agent in order to provide the expected level of service.

You also might want to investigate becoming a "work-out" specialist. These individuals work on real estate investments that have failed to meet their potential, and they deal with how the property can most effectively be liquidated and how creditors can recoup their investments. Although these professionals are often referred to as the "grave diggers" of the real estate profession, it was the area of greatest growth in the late 1980s. Financial expertise, rather than deal-making skills, are most important for this specialty. Work-out is a hot area for accountants, financial analysts and lawyers, who have had experience in the real estate market.

Women continue to make successful inroads into commercial real estate. Historically, the commercial field has been dominated by men. This has changed, particularly in the shopping center segment of commercial real estate. Women have been particularly effective in the leasing of shopping centers, in part because the customer base of retail establishments remains predominantly female. This area requires a particularly good understanding of issues affecting retailers, and are effective in structuring leases that meet their unique needs.

Breaking in

Entry into the residential real estate area requires a real estate license but does not require any specific level of formal education. You will find high school graduates and Ph.D.'s all successfully working in the field. Most individuals in commercial real estate have undergraduate degrees, and many have MBAs or law degrees as well.

The best way to break in is to apply directly to the firms in your area. Residential and commercial firms are listed in the yellow pages. In the interview the manager will focus on sales skills. Thus, individuals who have had some experience in selling have an advantage. However, if you can make a case for why you're interested in real estate and why you think you'd be good at it, some companies will give you a chance.

Some commercial real estate companies provide extensive in-house training and many colleges are offering classes on real estate. These may range from evening continuing education classes to programs leading to a master's degree in real estate. Classes often cover such subjects as environmental concerns, urban planning, real estate investment trusts and housing partnerships.

Compensation

Residential real estate agents earn 6 percent of the property's selling price as commission. The commission is split between the agent who represents the seller and the agent representing the buyer. The agents then split their percentages with the real estate agency they work for. The percentage that the agent keeps varies considerably. The real estate agency ReMax revolutionized the industry by recruiting experienced, successful agents and allowing them to keep 100 percent of their commissions. ReMax agents pay a fixed monthly fee to cover office overhead and administrative costs. This unique arrangement forced other agencies to pay higher percentages to their top agents lest they be recruited away by ReMax.

Earnings come from commissions, and it takes time to build up business. First-year compensation of $12,000 to $18,000 is common. An agent with five years of experience typically earns $30,000 to $50,000. There is no ceiling on earning potential and successful agents can earn well into the six figures. However, it takes time to get started, so be persistent.

Commercial real estate may pay first-year employees an annual salary of $12,000 to $30,000. After the first year, the salary is replaced by commissions. Successful commercial agents with five years of experience can earn $50,000 to $90,000. It is possible for commercial developers to earn $1 million or more.

Successful agents acquire a variety of perks, in addition to a larger percentage of the commission. Agencies zealously protect their star agents and offer them a variety of benefits, including automobile leases, car phones and country club memberships.

Career path

Although most individuals in real estate are more interested in doing deals and selling property then they are with career advancement, managerial opportunities do exist. A sales manager may supervise the activities of 5 to 10 agents and may be responsible for the training of new agents. Most managers have a minimum of five years of experience.

Some people work in real estate on a part-time basis. Once your reputation is established, it is possible to limit the number of clients you're working with. Thus, real estate is particularly appealing for people seeking to balance their lifestyles and careers.

Major employers: Who and where

The best opportunities in real estate are in the Southeast and Midwest. However, in virtually every city there are good opportunities. Try to focus on affluent suburbs or "corporate enclaves" where people are regularly moving in and out. In residential real estate, Century 21 is well-regarded for training, and ReMax is considered one of the better places for experienced agents. Both Coldwell Banker and Trammel Crow have good reputations in the commercial real estate field.

Resources

Some key employers

Century 21 Real Estate Corp.
2601 Southeast Main
Irvine, CA 92713
714-553-2100

Coldwell Banker, Inc.
27271 Las Ramblas
Mission Viejo, CA 92691
714-367-2121

ReMax Realty Associates
3425 Market Street
Camp Hill, PA 17011
717-761-6300

Trammel Crow Real Estate Investors
2001 Ross Avenue
Dallas, TX 75201
214-979-5451

Associations

National Association of Realtors
430 North Michigan Avenue
Chicago, IL 60611-4087
312-329-8200

National Association of Real Estate Companies
P.O. Box 958
Columbia, MD 21044
301-821-1614

Institute of Real Estate Management
430 North Michigan Avenue
Chicago, IL 60611
312-329-6000

International Real Estate Institute
8383 East Evans Road
Scottsdale, AZ 85260
602-998-8267

Publications

Commercial Property News
1515 Broadway
New York, NY 10036
212-869-1300

Real Estate Today
430 North Michigan Avenue
Chicago, IL 60611
312-329-8449

First Tuesday
Realty Publications, Inc.
P.O. Box 20068
Riverside, CA 92516
714-781-7300

Real Estate Magazine
415 North State Street
Chicago, IL 60610
312-644-7800

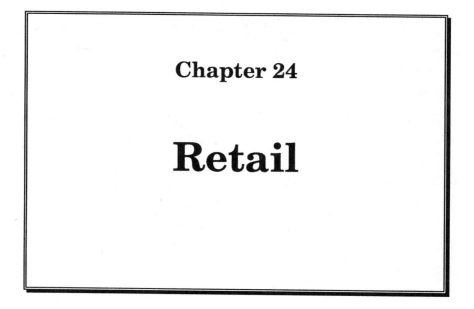

Chapter 24

Retail

Despite consolidations among the major retail chains in the 1980s, this is a field with a voracious appetite for people. Although the hours are often long and the initial pay modest, retail still employs a large number of recent college graduates. For those willing to make an investment, a career in retail can be highly rewarding.

Gone are the days when retail clerks merely sat behind the cash register and rang up purchases. The success of chains such as The Gap has shown retailers that to be competitive in the 1990s, customer service is king. Thus, retailing is often a very positive exposure to sales and customer service, and it can improve interpersonal skills.

What's hot and why

Retail is one of the largest employers of young people. It can provide valuable training, initial exposure to business and a lot of responsibility, even at entry level. The greatest opportunities in retail are in sales, buying, merchandising and operations.

Sales. Retail is ultimately all about sales. Although it's likely you'll be rotated through a series of assignments in your retailing career, you'll have to prove yourself in sales if you expect to progress.

In many ways retail sales is easier than many other types of sales. The customers come to you, seeking your expertise and knowledge of the product—whether they are purchasing shoes or sophisticated electronic equipment. The ability to establish credibility as a helpful resource is a critically important skill for the retail salesperson.

You must also know when to offer assistance and when to back away. Nothing bothers a customer more than a salesperson who hovers at the customer's elbow after being told that he or she is "just browsing." Successful salespeople take this as a sign to disappear, but make periodic checks. Although customers often don't want to be followed, they also hate having to hunt down a salesperson once they have made a decision or have a question. Top retail salespeople discretely observe what has caught the customer's eye and may comment on the product as they periodically check back.

These tips are often taught in training classes by many of the larger chains. Even if you eventually pursue a career outside of retail, the lessons learned in salesmanship and customer service are valuable in most future jobs.

Buying. While selling is critical for retail success, offering the right product lines is equally important. Deciding what the store will stock is the job of the buyers. Each year, buyers attend a number of shows in which the current product line is displayed. Buyers tend to specialize in a particular area, such as fashion, home furnishings or electronics. Their success depends upon their ability to identify what is new, hot and likely to catch the public's fancy.

This is often very difficult to predict. What is a hot fashion design in Paris may not sell well in Wichita. What 30-year-old men think will be the next hot toy may be quite different than the opinion of an 8-year-old. Buying is an area in which careers are quickly launched or quickly derailed. Individuals who demonstrate that they have a feel for what the buying public wants find themselves in great demand by competing retail chains.

Although many people briefly rotate through a tour in buying, those with an aptitude for it often request a permanent assignment. While the risks are great, top buyers are some of the most highly compensated executives in retailing.

Merchandising refers to how the product is displayed in the store or buying environment. Clothing that is attractively displayed on a mannequin will sell better than clothing lumped in a pile. Merchandisers also learn that mannequins are effective tools for selling entire outfits. Toy-store merchandisers know that if a child has an opportunity to play with a toy, the likelihood that Mom and Dad will purchase it is considerably greater. Good merchandisers know how to subtly influence the public's buying behavior.

Operations. Since the success of a retail chain is predicated upon the opening of new stores, major chains must train future managers. Since each chain is unique, there is considerable pressure to create a pipeline of candidates who can manage one, or many, stores. Operations, or multiple- store management, is often described as one of the most challenging and enjoyable jobs in retail.

As an area manager with three to five stores reporting to you, you are responsible for profit and loss, for hiring, firing, sales, profitability, administration and operations.

One of the things area managers enjoy is the diversity of their work. However, this does not minimize the pressure. Sucess can lead to jobs as district or regional managers, but failure to meet profit and sales goals often leads to dismissal. Oprations is where many retail chains draw their future senior executives from; therefore it is one of the most visible assignments within a chain.

Breaking in

Retail chains recruit extensively on college campuses, advertise opportunities in the newspaper, and interview candidates who apply in person. College degrees are preferred but exceptions are often made.

During the interview, the store manager will focus on your sales skills and leadership capabilities. Make sure you bring up any prior experience in sales, regardless of what the product was. Examples of leadership might include a fraternity or sorority presidency, shift management at a restaurant or being an athletic team captain. The interviewer will also question you on your ability to work weekends and evenings. Retail stores are open long hours, and as a new employee you'll have to be willing to work the less popular shifts. Since computers are used to monitor the movement of goods, familiarity with PCs is becoming more and more important.

Make sure you ask intelligent questions during the interview. There is no shortage of retail opportunities, so look for a company that is committed to your training and development. Ask specifically about what type of training you'll receive. Is it just an initial two-week, on-the-job program or is it formal and ongoing? Find out about the career path. How long will it take to become a store manager? What are the opportunities beyond that level? Speak to an employee at the same level you would start at.

Compensation

You must approach retail with a long-term career perspective. Yes, the money is initially low, but many chains have incentive programs that can make your total compensation, including bonuses and commissions, quite attractive. Moreover, middle-management jobs, in which you may be responsible for multiple stores, offer a lot of independence and an opportunity to earn a lucrative salary.

Starting salaries range from $13,000 to $25,000 and may include an employee discount of 10 to 25 percent on store goods. Experienced buyers, merchandisers and operations managers can earn $35,000 to $65,000. Earnings in the six figures are possible for multiple-store managers and buyers. Merchandisers tend to top out at around $55,000.

Career path

Most retail workers begin their careers in sales and progress into specialized areas. However, recent college graduates are sometimes hired to pursue a specific "track," such as buying. Whether you start out as a generalist or a specialist, most chains will try to expose you to a variety of departments. This early exposure is very helpful in developing a broad understanding of retail.

In five to seven years you may have begun to specialize in a particular area. Although you may move through a number of departments in the course of a career, it is important that you establish a reputation for excellence in a particular area within your first 10 years. This specialization can be an effective springboard to the more general management assignments down the road.

There are many routes to the top. If growth is a significant issue, the top people are often from the operations side of the business. If the chain has been criticized for not carrying current or popular items, someone from the buyer's function may assume leadership. Merchandisers become very important when goods aren't displayed tastefully or stores are perceived as crowded and dingy. Since retail tends to be youth-oriented, you can find many senior-level general managers in their 40s.

Major employers: Who and where

The top cities for retail are New York and Los Angeles, although good opportunities exist virtually everywhere in the nation. Some chains you might consider include: Bergdorf Goodman, The Bombay Company, Brooks Brothers, Brookstone Company, Carson Pirie Scott & Company, Carter Hawley Hale Stores, Cartier, Circuit City, Dayton Hudson, Dell Computer, Federated Department Stores, Filene's, The Gap, Hartmarx Company, Home Depot, Kinney Shoe, Kohl's Department Stores, Lechmere, Lord & Taylor, I. Magnin, May Department Stores, Montgomery Ward, Pep Boys, J.C. Penney, Polo/Ralph

Lauren, Saks Fifth Avenue, Scrivner's Inc., Service Merchandise, Southland Corp., Spencer Gifts, Sears, Tandy Corp., Toys R Us and Wal-Mart Stores. The National Retail Merchants Association, located at 100 West 31st Street, New York, NY 10001, may also provide you with additional information.

Resources

Some key employers

The Gap
900 Cherry Avenue
San Bruno, CA 94066
415-952-4400

Carter Hawley Hale Stores
444 Flower Street
Los Angeles, CA 90071
213-620-0150

Brooks Brothers
346 Madison Avenue
New York, NY 10017
212-682-8800

Cartier, Inc.
653 Fifth Avenue
New York, NY 10022
212-753-0111

Carson Pirie Scott & Company
36 South Wabash Avenue
Chicago, IL 60603
312-641-8000

The May Department Stores Company
611 Olive Street
St. Louis, MO 63101
314-342-6300

Associations

National Retail Federation
100 West 31st Street
New York, NY 10001
212-244-8780

National Retail Federation
100 West 31st Street
New York, NY 10001
212-244-8780

National Association of Retail Dealers of America
10 East 22nd Street
Lombard, IL 60148
312-953-8950

Menswear Retailers of America
2011 I Street NW, Suite 300
Washington, DC 20006
202-347-1932

Publications

Retail Information Systems News
1 West Hanover Avenue,
Randolph, NJ 07869
201-895-3300

Stores
100 West 31st Street
New York, NY 10001
212-244-8780

Chain Store Age Executive
425 Park Avenue
New York, NY 10022
212-756-5252

Chain Merchandiser
65 Crocker Avenue
Piedmont, CA 94611
415-547-4545

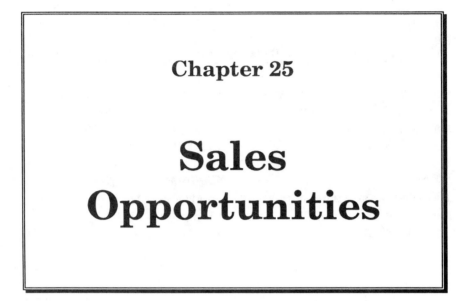

Chapter 25

Sales Opportunities

If you're motivated by the opportunity to earn a large income and work independently, sales may be the career for you. However, the old saying that a good salesperson can sell anything is obsolete. Today's salespeople are specialists who have an intimate knowledge of their product lines and customers.

The one component shared by most sales positions is the independent nature of the job. While the good news is that you don't have someone looking over your shoulder all the time, the bad news is that it can be lonely. You may spend a lot of time on the road. Although most sales organizations attempt to maintain employees' motivation through periodic sales meetings, you need the ability to function effectively by *yourself* to enjoy a sales career.

What draws most people to sales is money, or at least the prospect of making it. Most salespeople are paid a combination of base salary plus commissions, or bonuses. The highest paid salespeople receive most of their compensation in commissions. Sales is most satisfying for people who want their earnings to reflect how successfully they sell. While advertisements for sales jobs use colorful language such as "unlimited income opportunity," remember that there is no floor either.

Sales is a great career for the type of person who has little tolerance for office politics. What salespeople love the most is closing the deal. However, while you'll need to be aggressive, the most effective individuals are light-years away from the stereotypical used-car salesperson. In style and demeanor, successful sales agents are customer-focused and rarely the glib, fast-talking characters pictured in TV and movies.

In order to excel at sales, you have to be a good listener. The problem that most new salespeople have is that they are more interested in selling their products than in solving a customer's problem. You must learn to shut up and listen to your customer. This is hard when you've spent hours learning and memorizing the 13 reasons why your customer should buy your product.

Deciding whether sales is right for you is one thing. Deciding what to sell is even more confusing. After all, salespeople sell virtually everything. Some questions to ask yourself include: How often do you actually want to sell something? Some salespeople prefer to sell something every day, while others enjoy big-ticket items that they may only sell once or twice a year. The former might include stocks, while an example of the latter is jet airplanes.

What type of people do you want to call on? This is very important since you'll be spending a lot of time with prospective clients. If you don't like grocery stores, don't go to work for one of the consumer goods companies. These salespeople spend a great deal of time in stores working on display preparations and dealing with store buyers. Want to sell to highly educated professionals, such as doctors? Think about pharmaceutical sales.

What types of hobbies or special interests do you have? You might as well sell something in which you have a personal interest. Many stockbrokers entered that field out of an early interest in investments. Sports equipment manufacturers share a passion for the sports they represent.

Take the time to thoroughly investigate different fields before you make your decision. Since sales is increasingly a field of specialists, it may be difficult to transfer to another area once you've built up expertise in a particular field.

What's hot and why

Sales will always be one of the top career fields since everything must be sold. However, you can't simply offer the world's best mouse trap and expect everyone to beat a path to your door. You must identify potential buyers, explain the features and benefits of your trap, and overcome buyer reluctance to emptying the trap of dead rats. Hot area in sales include the following:

Medical products. Selling opportunities in this field have remained the most stable over the past few years and are expected to grow in double digits throughout the 1990s. This is good news for individuals who sell such products as operating room supplies and other medical equipment.

One of the most popular methods of entering the field is to join one of the large pharmaceutical or drug firms. However, don't think about going to work for one of these companies if you don't like school. Since new drugs are constantly being introduced, you'll spend a lot of time learning about your company's drugs, the competition's products, and how various drugs interact with each other. You'll also be enrolled in a concentrated training program in which you'll learn biology, physiology and chemistry. All of this training is critical if you are going to successfully interact with a physician.

Consumer products. Consumer products are defined as goods sold directly to the consumer through grocery or department stores. Within the consumer products field, sales positions in the food industry are growing the fastest. Many of these positions are staffed by students directly out of college, although companies often hire experienced individuals who have an impressive sales background in another field.

This field is good for people interested in merchandising. Sales reps address issues such as how products can be positioned on the shelf to easily catch the customer's eye and how displays can increase sales. More than ever before, high technology is used to build sales. Examples include shopping carts with video TV screens and hidden sensors that beep or signal the customer as he or she approaches the shelves. The retail outlets are becoming high-tech, and the consumer goods sales reps are at the forefront of the innovations.

Industrial products. Selling products such as pumps or valves may not be glamorous, but it is a good area to work in if you have a technical orientation and enjoy seeing projects built. You may be selling to building engineers, construction supervisors or facilities managers. Sales to the construction trade account for a large percentage of this business. As the economy picks up and housing sales increase, selling to the commercial and residential construction trade will again offer excellent opportunities.

Business products. This field is one of the largest recruiters of college graduates going into sales. Business products refers to everything from copiers and fax machines to paper clips and other staples necessary for running a business. This field has an excellent reputation for training individuals on sales techniques. Companies such as Xerox have set the standard for providing high-quality sales training. While sales of business products is competitive, it can be rewarding.

High technology/computers. As computers become a part of our daily lives, opportunities for sales careers will grow. Most of the positions involve calling on large corporate clients, assessing their computing needs and recommending software and hardware systems. The sales rep may also assist in the installation of the equipment. The job requires a great amount of technical knowledge and is one of the more service-oriented sales positions. Similar to pharmaceuticals, the technology is continually changing, which makes the job intellectually stimulating. Most of the hiring in the 1990s is anticipated to occur at the smaller start-up organizations.

Breaking in

It's not surprising that the key factor in a job candidate is sales ability. This sometimes results in some bizarre recruiting practices, particularly at the entry level. Stress-inducing questions such as "Can you sell me this pen?" are common in sales recruiting. The trick to answering this type of question is to think "features" and "benefits." The features of the pen might be that it's a nice color, retracts easily and holds standard size ink cartridges. A benefit might be: "If you buy 50 pens from me today, I'll throw in an additional 10 pens for free." The key is not to get thrown when this question comes at you.

Pharmaceutical, consumer goods and high-tech companies prefer a four-year degree. However, exceptions are sometimes made. Although you may be able to break in without a college degree, you'll find that your career is limited.

Hiring is continual, although some industries experience a slowdown during the summer. A large percentage of jobs are advertised in newspapers. It's sometimes difficult to separate the good opportunities from the junk. If you see an ad that states "Can you get by on $100,000 per year?" you're probably looking at an opportunity to sell real estate that is currently underwater. A better approach is to identify companies in which you have a specific interest and apply directly. Rather than asking for the personnel manager, ask to speak with the area sales manager. You'll discover that it's easy to get this person on the phone. Most sales managers are willing to meet with you since they never know when one of their reps will be promoted or transferred, or will decide to quit. Thus, savvy sales managers like to have an inventory of applicants so they can cut down on recruiting time.

If you have sales experience, you may find the recruiting firms that specialize in sales helpful. Two national firms, Sales Consultants and Sales Recruiters, have a handle on what's going on in the market. There are also good local firms in most cities. Get recommendations from people who got their jobs through recruiting firms. The recruiting firms are a better resource for people with experience than for those who are just starting out.

The hiring process for salespeople places a lot of emphasis on interviewing skills, style and image. You should look like the client you're going to be calling on. Thus, if you're applying at IBM, dress in a conservative dark suit. If you're applying to sell industrial construction equipment, slacks and a blazer might be more appropriate.

Be prepared to answer some challenging questions: "Why are you interested in sales?" "Why do you think you would be good at sales?" "How do you know you'd be good at sales?" And the ever popular, "Sell me this pen."

Err on the side of aggressiveness after your interview. Many sales managers will gauge your sales ability by how effective you are in selling *yourself*. Be persistent, but not obnoxious. Stay in regular contact. If the sales manager says he will contact you in a week and you don't hear from him or her, follow up with a polite call or note. Remember that a lot of sales interviewing is done in anticipation of future staffing needs, which may not arise for several months.

Compensation

The most highly paid salespeople receive the bulk of their earnings in commissions. A top sales rep with 8 to 10 years of experience can earn $100,000 in many industries.

Starting salaries in high-tech/computer sales range from $15,000 for an individual with little formal education to $35,000 for a degreed engineer. Experienced reps earn an average salary of $60,000. Base salaries vary enormously. Normal payout is 40 percent salary and 60 percent commissions.

Compensation in the medical products field starts at $22,000 to $26,000. Experienced sales reps' salaries range from $35,000 to $70,000. Typically, 80 percent of the compensation is salary, with the remainder in bonuses.

Entry-level compensation in consumer goods is about $25,000 and often includes a company car. An experienced sales rep earns between $30,000 and $60,000, 85 percent as salary.

Earnings of $85,000 and more are possible for experienced salespeople in the office products field. However, with this potential there is also a degree of risk, since 80 to 90 percent of your earnings are often from commissions. Individuals who are confident in their sales abilities and who desire to have their earnings based on their production find business product sales the most rewarding area.

A sales career in the industrial products field typically begins by working as an inside sales rep, handling phone orders, or working in the customer service area. These initial jobs provide the product training necessary for success in outside sales. Salaries for entry-level jobs begin around $18,000. Experienced sales reps earn around $50,000, although the more technical the product, the greater the earnings potential.

Career path

A lot of CEOs of major corporations began their careers in sales. Conversely, a large number of sales reps decide that working as a rep is all they want to do. Regardless of your goals, most sales careers require a commitment of a minimum of three to five years of field work. After that time, the opportunity to go into management is often offered to the reps who display the most potential.

A common organizational structure includes district sales managers, area managers, regional managers and divisional managers. The head of the field sales organization reports to a corporate VP of sales, who usually reports to the president of the company. If you are interested in pursuing the management track, be prepared for frequent relocations. For many years the joke among the IBM sales staff was that the company's initials stood for "I've Been Moved."

Major employers: Who and where

Although virtually every company has a sales department, not all companies have a good training program, which is crucial at the early stages. Companies with a reputation for excellence in this area include: IBM, Xerox, General Electric, Procter & Gamble, Kraft, Inc., General Foods Corp., Hilti,

Baxter, Travenol, Merck & Company, Inc., Johnson & Johnson, and Abbott Laboratories.

Local recruiting firms that specialize in sales can give you insights into the best opportunities in town. If you don't want to leave your current location, focus on smaller companies or firms that have headquarters in your city. Your chamber of commerce can provide you with a list of the major employers in your city.

Resources

Some key employers

General Electric
3135 Easton Turnpike
Fairfield, CT 06431
203-373-2028

Kraft, Inc.
6410 Poplar Avenue
Memphis, TN 38119
901-766-2100

General Foods Corp.
250 North Street
White Plains, NY 10625
914-335-2500

Merck & Company, Inc.
P.O. Box 2000
Rahway, NJ 07065
201-574-4000

IBM
Old Orchard Road
Armonk, NY 10504
914-765-1900

Procter & Gamble
One Procter & Gamble Plaza
Cincinnati, OH 45202
513-983-6293

Associations

**National Association for
Professional Saleswomen**
P.O. Box 2606
Novato, CA 94948
415-898-2606

**Sales and Marketing
Executives International**
Statler Office Tower, #458
Cleveland, OH 44115
216-771-6650

**Professional Salespersons
of America**
100 Maria Circle NW
Albuquerque, NM 87184
505-897-4568

**National Council of
Salesmen's Organizations**
225 Broadway, Room 515
New York, NY 10007
212-349-1707

Publications

Personal Selling Power
P.O. Box 5467
Fredricksburg, VA 22403
703-752-7000

Sales Motivation
1640 Fifth Street
Santa Monica, CA 90401
213-395-0234

Agency Sales Magazine
P.O. Box 3467
Laguna Hills, CA 92654
714-859-4040

Sales & Marketing Management
Bill Communications, Inc.
633 Third Avenue
New York, NY 10017
212-986-4800

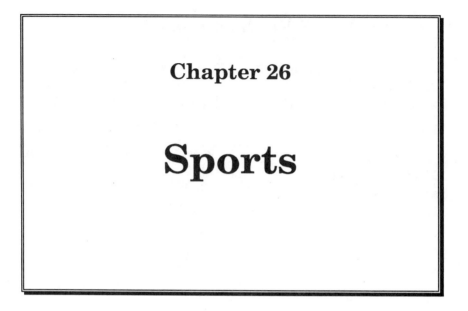

Chapter 26

Sports

Make no mistake about it, sports is big business. While the most visible aspect of the industry is on the playing field, the success of business depends on the savvy of a variety of professionals who work *behind* the scenes.

What's hot and why

The sports business now grosses more than $20 billion a year and continues to grow. With the public's increased interest in such sports as volleyball, billiards, boxing, golf, racquetball, rugby and surfing, sports has become one of the nation's growth businesses.

Sports offers a variety of career options that draw upon a diversity of skills and interests. Working as an agent, serving a professional franchise or representing an equipment manufacturer are three of the hottest opportunities in sports.

Sports agents. The agency business is dominated by four major firms: ICM, ProServ, Advantage International and

International Management Group. Among professional athletes, word quickly spreads about which agents and agencies make the best deals. While there are many individual agents who may represent one or two athletes, most of the top athletes are represented by one of these large firms.

The role of the agent can best be summarized as having two main components, signing and holding. You have to be good at getting and keeping players if you are going to be successful as an agent. Since the agent is the conduit between the team and the athlete, it is a critical position. Few athletes can negotiate for themselves, and the agent wields a great deal of power. As the number of professional athletes continues to grow, there will be need for agents who can represent them. However, the job requires a great amount of aggressiveness and tact.

Franchises. Jobs with professional franchises are considered some of the best in the industry. As major and minor league teams continue to expand and new leagues are formed, opportunities with the franchises are also expected to expand.

Franchises tend to be family-owned businesses. Many people don't understand franchises and have little knowledge about the jobs that are available. The first step is to think about your skills and what you can contribute to the job. Nobody will hire you just because you're interested in sports.

The two hot areas for employment in the franchises are in marketing and facility management. Marketing has become increasingly specialized as teams develop specific programs to attract various segments of the population. The marketing department puts together promotions to draw kids, senior citizens, business executives and other groups to the ball park. Much of the analysis is done by computer, and promotions are publicized through direct-mail campaigns.

A noticeable trend among professional sports teams is to own, or be responsible for the management of, the ball park. Individuals with a background in facilities management are in demand by the professional teams. Jobs in this area include managing security, organizing maintenance and directing the technical aspects of a first-class operation.

Equipment manufacturers. Finally, many of the rapidly growing equipment manufacturers offer some interesting careers for people drawn to the sports industry. These companies include Wilson Sporting Goods, Nike, Reebok, Rawlings and Riddell.

Equipment manufacturing is a business of identifying trends quickly, and providing a product nationwide. The manufacturing industry depends on marketing, production and distribution expertise for its survival.

Breaking in

Sports agents. Most agents break into the business by representing a particular athlete. Often this is a player who the agent-to-be met in college. While the physical skills of the college athlete may be well-developed, his or her understanding of the business aspects of a sports career are often limited.

If you've already missed out on the opportunity to befriend a college athlete, work on developing a skill that would be of benefit to an agency. This might be a knowledge of contracts or a creative marketing idea that could involve athletes during their off-seasons. The point is that you must have something to offer, aside from an interest in becoming an agent.

Another method of entering the field is to volunteer for a nonpaid internship while in school. These internships are often easier to obtain than you might imagine. For example, Pro-Serv, a leading sports management firm, sponsors events such as the AT&T Tennis Challenge and the Pizza Hut One-on-One Basketball Program. While you won't get paid, you will have an opportunity to make contacts and acquire valuable experience by assisting with these events.

Breaking into sports, like any other glamour business, depends greatly upon contacts. Starting your networking while in school can give you a major lead over the competition when you begin looking for a full-time job.

Legal training is the most common background for an agent since much of an agent's work involves contract negotiation. However, you do not need to have a law background in order to be a successful agent. The most important skill is the ability to market an athlete. This requires identifying potential sponsors and securing product endorsements. Obtaining endorsements for a client is the key to holding an athlete.

If you really want to become an agent, it's a good idea to think about what sport you want to represent, since agents tend to specialize. Sports agents agree that the most difficult sport for an agent is football. Relatively few players are recruited into the professional ranks each year, and the playing career is less than five years. Best type of athlete to represent? Professional golfers. The popularity of the Seniors Professional Tour underscores the fact that golfers can continue to perform and earn substantial incomes for decades.

Franchises. If you're interested in working for one of your local sports franchises, buy a program the next time you're at a game. Read the brief biographies of the business people in the franchise. These are the individuals to whom you'll want to send your resume.

Experience in direct mail or in one of the many computer analysis software packages could make you very attractive to a franchise. In many cases you may be hired to work on one specific project. If that works out you may be brought back to work on additional projects, and ultimately a full-time job may materialize. Sports franchises are big believers in testing people before making a commitment of full-time employment.

Equipment manufacturing. These businesses often look for people who have an expertise in marketing, finance or distribution, even if it is in another industry. As the manufacturing process is moved out of the United States, people with a knowledge of import/export and raw material sourcing are in demand. Since much of the manufacturing is now in Asia and Mexico, the ability to speak Spanish, Chinese, or Japanese would make you a very attractive candidate.

If you don't have specific skills in one of these areas, the most common entry point is sales. Equipment manufacturers such as Nike and Reebok like people who have sold their products for one of the large retail chains or sporting goods chains. Thus, before you turn your nose up to the retail shoe business, realize that it may lead to opportunities beyond the shopping mall.

Compensation

A lot of people break into sports areas through unpaid internships or volunteer work.

An agent's compensation is based on a percentage of what his or her clients earn. Representing a million-dollar athlete can dramatically change an agent's life. Earnings in the $20,000 range are common for the first few years. However, a successful agent with 8 to 10 years of experience will usually earn between $50,000 and $150,000. A handful of agents at the top of their careers earn more than $500,000.

Opportunities with the professional sports franchises range from $14,000 to $50,000. The latter positions are usually finance jobs held by recent MBA graduates. After 10 to 15 years, you may become a marketing or operations department head and earn $30,000 to $90,000. Few positions, aside from the general manager of the franchise, pay more than $100,000.

Positions with the equipment manufacturers often start around $25,000 to $30,000, unless you have a specific skill such as knowledge of a foreign language or manufacturing. After five to eight years, successful managers typically earn $40,000 to $80,000. The head of a department, sometimes a vice president, can earn $80,000 to $125,000, plus bonuses.

Career path

Agents generally aren't interested in management. Their goal is to represent the most prominent athletes and negotiate increasingly larger contracts for their clients. An agent may begin his or her career by representing one client who earns $100,000. As the agent's reputation grows, he may develop a stable of 10 clients, each of whom is earning $250,000. At the peak of the career, the agent may represent 20 clients, each of whom earns $1 million.

The career path in a professional sports franchise may involve rotating through a diversity of assignments. Since franchises tend to be family-owned, career progression is relatively

214

informal. After 10 to 15 years, you can expect to be responsible for the overall activities of a particular area, such as marketing or finance.

Equipment manufacturers enjoy a more traditional career path. You'll typically start in sales, accounting or manufacturing. This assignment usually lasts two to five years. Success will often lead to a supervisor's job, in which you will be responsible for the activities of 5 to 10 workers. Progression up the ladder leads to assignments such as department manager, director and vice president. It usually takes 12 to 15 years to become a vice president. People tend to spend the majority of their careers in a particular area, such as marketing or accounting, although temporary assignments to other areas are common for developmental purposes. Most general managers have spent considerable time in the marketing and manufacturing sectors.

Major employers: Who and where

Top talent agencies include: Advantage International, Washington, D.C.; ICM, Los Angeles; International Management Group, Cleveland Ohio; ProServ, Arlington Va.; Career Sports Management, Atlanta; Championship Group, Atlanta; Pro Player Reps, Dallas; and Bob Wolf Associates, Boston.

Equipment manufacturers include: Adidas, Warren, N.J.; Avia, Portland, Ore.; Cramer Products, Inc., Gardner, Kan.; Danskin, York, Pa.; Dunlop Slazenger, Greenville, S.C.; Gold's Gym Inc., Venice, Calif.; Izod/Lacoste, Reading, Pa.; Keds, Cambridge, Mass.; Nautilus Corporation, Independence, Va.; Nike, Beaverton, Ore.; Prince Manufacturing Company, Inc., Lawrenceville, N.J.; Raleigh Cycle Co., Kent, Wash.; Rawlings Sporting Goods, Fenton, Mo.; Reebok International Ltd., Stoughton, Mass.; Spalding Sports Worldwide, Chicopee, Mass.; and Wilson Sporting Goods, River Grove, Ill.

From professional sports franchises, you can choose from baseball, basketball, football, hockey and more. There are teams located in virtually every major city.

Resources

Some key employers

ProServ
1101 Wilson Boulevard
Arlington, VA 22209
703-276-3030

Cramer Products, Inc.
(athletic training supplies)
153 West Warren
Gardner, KS 66030
913-884-7511

Danskin
305 State Street
York, PA 17403
717-852-6100

Nike, Inc.
1 Bowerman Drive
Beaverton, OR 97005
503-641-6453

**Prince Manufacturing
Company, Inc.**
3 Princess Road
Lawrenceville, NJ 08648
201-896-2500

Reebok International Ltd.
100 Technology Center Drive
Stoughton, MA 02072
617-341-5087

Associations

**Sporting Goods
Manufacturers Association**
200 Castlewood Road
North Palm Beach, FL 33408
407-842-4100

**National League of
Professional Baseball Clubs**
350 Park Avenue, 18th Floor
New York, NY 10022
212-826-7700

**National Basketball
Association**
645 Fifth Avenue, 15th Floor
New York, NY 10022
212-826-7000

National Football League
410 Park Avenue
New York, NY 10022
212-758-1500

Publications

Sporting Goods Dealer
2 Park Avenue
New York, NY 10016
212-779-5000

Sport Magazine
8490 Sunset Boulevard
Los Angeles, CA 90069
213-854-2250

Sports Illustrated
1271 Avenue of the Americas
New York, NY 10020
212-522-1212

The Sporting News
1212 North Lindbergh Boulevard
St. Louis, MO 63132
314-997-7111

Index

Where the Jobs Are

Where the Jobs Are

Where the Jobs Are